BIOLOGICALLY
BANKRUPT

BIOLOGICALLY BANKRUPT
...Sins of the Fathers

Adair Sanders

Outskirts Press, Inc.
Denver, Colorado

Outskirts Press, Inc.
http://www.outskirtspress.com

ISBN: 978-1-4327-6637-5

Outskirts Press and the "OP" logo are trademarks belonging to Outskirts Press, Inc.

PRINTED IN THE UNITED STATES OF AMERICA

This is a true story.

Contents

Prologue

I buried my father on a beautiful day in April. Forest Hills Cemetery is an old cemetery resting at the foot of Lookout Mountain. In the spring, like the day when I buried my father, Forest Hills is a riot of color – azaleas, spirea, dogwoods, and jonquils. Life running riot over the sleeping dead. Generations of Chattanoogans are buried at Forest Hills, with monuments and statuary bearing the names of those old founding families as well as the Carpetbagger families who came after the Civil War and made their fortunes off the less-fortunate local survivors.

Of course, most people had quit drawing that distinction years previous, with my father being "an" or maybe even "the" exception. My father was rabid about the "old South" and one of the biggest racists and bigots I have ever known.

My entire life, I heard about how the South had been screwed in the War Between the States, how Yankees (anyone living above the Mason-Dixon line) were stupid, that integration was sinful and was being forced on "us" by the evil federal government, and that Martin Luther King was a communist. When JFK was assassinated my father actually cheered.

One of my father's most cherished treasures was a picture of the Chattanooga Ku Klux Klan standing around my great-grandfather's grave in their outfits. My father would proudly tell me who the disguised spooks were – allegedly important pillars of Chattanooga society. My father had all sorts of "true stories" about rampaging "niggers" after the end of the War Between the States, and how the KKK had been necessary to protect white women and keep the "niggers" in their place. Of course, when I or my children would confront my father about his racism, he would indignantly point out the "niggers" who were his individual friends. He would say, "Well, there are a few good ones, but as a race 'niggers' are just savages from the jungle." My father would make these comments in front of anyone. Frankly, I am amazed no one ever shot him.

Anyway, to return to the story, it was ironic that my father was actually buried at Forest Hills. My father placed great store on appearances and social status. To that end, Forest Hills would have seemed the logical place for him to spend eternity. After all, every Protestant or Catholic family of note in Chattanooga was buried at Forest Hills. This is not to say that unrenowned or unremarkable people were not also buried at Forest Hills, because of course they were. However, if you were anyone in life, and you weren't Jewish, then you certainly expected to end up in Forest Hills.

My parents argued about this for years. My mother's family was buried at Forest Hills. My father's family was buried at Greenwood Cemetery on the other side of town. My mother was adamantly opposed to being buried with my father's family at Greenwood Cemetery. She thought Greenwood Cemetery was a lower-class cemetery, and she despised her mother-in-law. I am not sure which mattered more to my mother – the possibility of being buried in a lower-class cemetery, or the thought of being buried with my father's mother. From the time my parents married until the time my father's mother died, there were three people in my parents' marriage instead of two. After spending thirty-plus years in a such a dysfunctional dynamic, I could understand why my mother didn't want to end up being ultimately buried as a threesome.

My father was equally adamant about not being buried at Forest Hills. My father had always looked down on my mother's family. Just like my mother despised my father's mother, my father despised my mother's mother. Many was the time my father would start on one of his rants about my mother's "less-than" family. No matter how the tirade would start, it always ended up with my father talking about how my mother's mother had tried to break up his marriage, how my mother's family "didn't have a pot to piss in" and how glad he was when "that old bitch" died.

When I was growing up I learned early on that there was only one rule that mattered in our house. That rule was that my father was always right. If Jesus Christ had appeared and told my father that he was wrong, my father would have told Jesus that He didn't know what He was talking about. There was no arguing with my father. No one's opinion mattered except his. So it was clear to me that Greenwood Cemetery was going to be the final resting place of my parents.

I was wrong. It was not until I was an adult myself that I began to understand my father's story and to see how his demons shaped his marriage to my mother, his role as a parent to me and my brother, his life as a businessman, and overriding everything, his need to be needed and to look good to others.

My father was deeply insecure. To make himself feel better he "talked bad" about other people all the time, telling my brother and me about their personal and financial defects. Most of these people were customers of the bank where my father worked, and I can only imagine what his bank customers would have done had they known that my father told us about their loans, how much they owed, how much they earned, etc. to justify why my father would not play golf (a waste of time) or why we could not join the local swimming club (a waste of money).

The second way in which my father tried to combat his insecurity was by playing the martyr role. This actually accomplished two goals. First, it met his need to be needed; and second, it made him look good to others. My father played the martyr role three times. First he was a martyr for his mother. My father had a most abnormal relationship with his mother. After his father died, when my father was in his second year of college, my father became his mother's surrogate husband for thirty-some years. The relationship between my father and his mother molded the relationship my father had with my mother, my brother, and me. We were distant seconds.

My father's second role as martyr was perfect for him. Miss Catherine was an eccentric millionaire who had been a friend of my mother's since childhood. Sometime in her fifties, Miss Catherine decided to take to her bed to die. This was not as odd as it sounds. Southern women had engaged in this kind of behavior for years. If you decided you didn't like how life was turning out, you either started drinking or you just went to bed. At any rate, Miss Catherine stayed in bed for about twenty years before she finally did die. During this time my father became Miss Catherine's "boy," although he certainly gave himself a much more elevated status. He hired her sitters, he collected her rents, he managed her accounts, he directed her charitable giving. As with his mother, all of my father's time and attention was directed to Miss Catherine's needs. Miss Catherine was a harsh and difficult taskmaster. The worse Miss Catherine treated my father, the better he liked it. It made him look so good to be taking such good care of such a mean and pitiful old woman.

The third and last role my father played as martyr was as caretaker for my mother after her second stroke. My mother had two strokes two years apart. She had a full recovery from the first one, so my father was able to return to taking care of Miss Catherine and her money. However, my mother's second stroke significantly incapacitated her physically. In fact, it was so serious that the doctors thought she might not survive. My mother did survive but was never able to regain independent living. This last role was the best one for filling my father's needs. What a loving and devoted husband he appeared to be. No one ever heard the vile and hateful words he said to my mother. She was his captive and he made the most of it until he died.

However, I digress. After my mother had the second stroke, and before we realized she would survive it, my father decided to buy burial plots at Forest Hills so he could bury mother there. My father never thought my mother would outlive him. Since my father never did anything that did not have a payoff for him, my guess is he thought he would bury mother at Forest Hills, be praised for giving his wife this final gift – i.e., really look good – and then later move her to Greenwood Cemetery after everything quieted down.

Things didn't work out the way my father planned. My mother survived the second stroke and he got cancer. He was dead ninety days after the diagnosis. I am sure he was pissed as hell, not so much for getting cancer, but because it wasn't going to work out the way he had planned. And so on a beautiful day in April I buried my father in Forest Hills Cemetery. And I was glad he was dead.

McKenzie Street

From the time I was born until I was in the second grade, we lived in an upstairs apartment at my father's mother's house. My Grandmother Margaret lived in the old home place, a big white two-story frame house with a huge covered porch that wrapped around three of the four sides of the house. The house was high on a hill on a sloping three-acre property. There were apple trees, a lighted badminton court, a concrete shuffleboard court, and the perfect climbing tree for a small child -- an old mimosa. Around the perimeter of the property on the McKenzie Street side was a high stone wall. Even though it was forbidden, I loved to walk along the top of that wall. It was fun and dangerous. In the front yard was a goldfish pond, fifteen feet in diameter. Although by the time I was born my grandmother no longer kept fish or water in it, it was still great fun to run up and down the sides of that concrete pond. There was even an old green concrete frog guarding the edge.

Framing the driveway were ancient fig trees. Those trees were great bee attractors in the summer, but the fruit they yielded made the best preserves. Every summer my grandmother and her maid Ella would make applesauce from the apples in her orchard and fig preserves from the figs on those bee trees. Ella would attach the apple corer to the edge of the kitchen table and I would watch in fascination as that magic device turned the apple round and round and pulled off the peel in long red stripes. I remember that there would be pots of figs and pots of apples smelling heavenly and boiling away, eventually dissolving into chunky sugary masses which would be poured into glass jars and sealed for enjoyment later in the year.

My mother's first problem was that she married my father after dating him for only one month, and before she had any idea who he really was. After they married my father tricked my mother into moving in to the McKenzie Street house by promising her that it was only temporary. During the Depression my grandparents had removed the interior staircase and put in an outside staircase so they could rent out the upstairs of their home for additional income. Although my grandparents recovered themselves financially after the Depression, they left the upstairs apartment separate. When my parents married they were waiting for an apartment to open up in a complex where many of their couple friends lived. My father assured my mother that they would only be living with his mother for few months until an apartment became available. What a lie.

My mother was a war widow. She had married the love of her life at nineteen and was a widow by twenty-three or twenty-four. After her first husband died she moved back in with her parents and took a job. She was a beautiful woman and she had her pick of suitors. In fact, at some point she became engaged to a dentist and was even buying furniture for the house she would be living in after they married when something happened and the engagement was suddenly off. My mother never discussed what happened to cause her to call off her engagement, but shortly thereafter she met my father and thirty days later they were married.

My mother quickly found herself pregnant with me. She also quickly realized she had made a terrible mistake in marrying my father. My father was incapable of being married to my mother because, for all intents and purposes, he was already married to his own mother. Every day when my father came home from work, he first stopped downstairs to visit with his mother. After spending time with her he would eventually go upstairs to my mother. My father refused to pay for a separate telephone line. He told my mother that having a separate phone line was unnecessary and a waste of money. (My mother and the rest of us would hear my father's favorite mantra "a waste of money" for over fifty years.) Whenever my mother received a telephone call my Grandmother Margaret would pick up the downstairs phone and listen to my mother's call to determine who was calling my mother and what the person was calling about. If my mother needed to use the telephone she had to ask my grandmother for permission to make sure that my grandmother did not want to use the phone herself.

My mother finally told my father she wanted a divorce. I can only imagine how hellish her life must have been for my mother to ask for a divorce in the early 1950s. Divorce was unheard of at that time. Nice women did not become divorcees. My father told my mother that if she tried to leave him he would "ruin" her - - that he would take me away from her and he would make sure she never saw me again. We were his possessions and, by God, he was going to keep us. Plus, if my mother got a divorce it would make my father look bad. Above all, he could not permit that to happen.

I, of course, was oblivious to all of this. I was not, however, oblivious to my father's rules.

One of those rules was with whom I was permitted to play. My Grandmother Margaret's house was in East Chattanooga. East Chattanooga was not the social hub of Chattanooga. It was a lower-middle-class and working-class neighborhood. Even though my father had grown up in East Chattanooga, he had gone to a private military school beginning in the ninth grade. In his mind, this gave him some sort of social status. My father conveniently ignored the fact that the only reason his parents could afford to send him to that school was because his mother was a teacher and had obtained a teacher's discount on the tuition. In reality, my father's family was nothing special. His mother was a teacher and his father was the manager of a fertilizer plant.

My mother, on the other hand, simply considered the neighborhood, and therefore its inhabitants, to be lower-class. She was horrified that circumstances had reduced her to living in an apartment above her mother-in-law in East Chattanooga. The circumstances in which my mother found herself were absolutely mortifying and humiliating for her.

The end result was that both my father and my mother – for totally different reasons -- considered themselves superior to their neighbors and as a consequence I was not allowed to play with any of the neighborhood children. I remember quite clearly wanting to play with the little girl a few doors down. Although I can't remember now what was actually said to me, I understood that my mother considered that girl and her family "inappropriate". Years later I discovered that the reason the little girl and her family were "inappropriate" was because the father worked a blue collar job. So, besides seeing my cousins off and on, I did not play with other children until I started kindergarten.

Another rule I learned was that no matter what happened, it was my fault. One of the best illustrations of this rule in action is the dog bite incident. I must have been about four years old. My mother and I were at the vet with our dog. A man in the waiting room had a beautiful German Shepherd with him. I went up to the man and asked him if I could pet his dog. He told me yes. When I reached out to pet the dog, the dog bit me. Because the dog had not been recently vaccinated for rabies, the vet quarantined the dog to make certain he was not infected. The vet told my mother that if the dog tested positive for rabies I would have to take the preventive shots.

When my mother and I returned home, I ran to my grandmother's kitchen to hide from my father. I knew he would be furious and that it would be my fault. Sure enough, when he got home from work and found out what happened he came storming into my grandmother's kitchen yelling for me. He found me trying to squeeze myself behind the refrigerator. He was irate. He screamed at me that if I had to have rabies shots he was going to "beat my ass." And he meant it. It did not matter that I had asked permission to pet the dog. It did not matter that the dog's owner told me I could pet the animal. It was my fault that I had been bitten and it would be my fault if my father had to spend his money on rabies shots for me. It never occurred to me to be afraid of taking fourteen rabies shots. The only thing I was afraid of was my father.

My brother actually chose to later endure fourteen rabies shots rather than be the target of our father's rage. When my brother was eight or nine years old he tried to catch a chipmunk. The chipmunk, being quicker than my brother and in fear of its life, quickly chomped on my brother's hand in order to effect an escape. My brother was well aware of what awaited him if he told my father what had happened. So he lied and told my parents that he was playing with his trucks on the driveway and the chipmunk had just run over and bitten him. Everyone assumed the chipmunk was rabid since it had bitten my brother without provocation. Rabies shots are extraordinarily painful. My brother could have stopped the shots at any time by telling my father that the chipmunk had bitten him in self-defense. He said nothing. The fear of my father was greater than the pain of fourteen rabies shots.

I don't know how my mother was able to finally convince my father to move out of the McKenzie Street house. I believe she cut him off sexually for three years after he threatened to take me away from her. I guess she didn't want to give him any more children to hold hostage. But eventually she got pregnant again and my brother Dan was born. Maybe it was having two children in that tiny upstairs apartment that made my father agree to move to a house of our own. Or maybe Grandmother Margaret got tired of hearing us running around over her head. Whatever the motivation, when I was seven and my brother was three we left the house on McKenzie Street and moved into a home of our own. My father did not, however, leave his mother. It just looked that way.

Little Dickie

As I have said, Grandmother Margaret was a school teacher. She taught seventh grade English for twenty-five years until she saw integration coming her way. My grandmother was typical of a woman of her class growing up in the South in the early 1900s. In her mind, "the Nigras" were not her equal and there was no way she was going to have "Nigras" in her class. So she retired.

After I was grown I would occasionally meet people who had been her students. I learned that she had been a difficult teacher who was feared, disliked, or both by most of her students. I also learned that she constantly talked to her students about my father, to whom she referred as "Little Dickie." The irony of that name is not lost on me, and I am sure it was not lost on my father growing up.

Pictures of my grandmother as a young married woman depict a short, plain, and overweight girl. Pictures of my grandfather depict the polar opposite. My grandfather was a tall, lean, mustachioed, and devilishly handsome man. He died years before I was born so I never knew him. I was mesmerized by his pictures. He was so different-looking from anyone else in my family and he seemed to be enjoying some sort of exotic life -- always standing in a rakish manner with his pipe, or on his speed boat, or in croquet whites.

Of course, my grandfather actually was enjoying an exotic life.

My grandmother and grandfather had a shotgun marriage, and after my father was born my grandparents entered into an agreed marriage of convenience. In exchange for my grandmother turning a blind eye to my grandfather's other life, my grandfather, for all intents and purposes, literally gave my father to my grandmother. My grandfather lived at the McKenzie Street house, and I am sure he kept up some sort of minimal appearances. However, his real life was with his mistresses, of whom he had several for the rest of his life. This was no secret. One of my father's cousins pointed out one of the women to my mother in public several years after she and my father married. I have no idea whether my father ever knew about his father's other life. It seems impossible that he could not have known, or that the knowledge that his father had chosen other women over his son would not have had a significant emotional impact on my father.

Life for my father in his formative years was difficult. From elementary school through high school, my father was required to sit at the kitchen table every night after dinner with his mother while she watched him do his homework. He had to take off his shoes when he entered the house, and he could not eat unless he was sitting at the kitchen table. The house rules were very rigid. My grandmother did not like anything to be out of place, and she despised dirt. Everything in my father's bedroom had to be perfectly in place. God forbid the bed should be unmade or dirty clothes left on the floor. There was no room for my father to be a boy in my grandmother's house.

There was also no opportunity in my grandmother's house for my father to learn how to be a man.

My grandmother required my father to take tap dancing lessons and to perform in elaborate costumes at public events throughout his high school years. In pictures I have seen of my father while dressed in his dance costume I see a petulant young man with anger barely contained beneath the surface of his face. That picture speaks a thousand words. Here was a young man on the cusp of adulthood completely castrated by his mother.

My grandmother also forbade my father from playing contact sports. She was afraid he would get hurt. Instead she required him to play the clarinet in the school band. This was another humiliation for my father. In his world, real men played sports – football in particular. They certainly did not play the clarinet. Playing in the band was not for real men. Yet that is exactly where my father found himself – dancing in ridiculous costumes, playing in the school band, and forbidden to engage in any athletic activities.

When I was growing up, my father would show my brother and me a few dance steps, and laugh at himself, but I never saw the clarinet anywhere. Maybe Fred Astaire and Gene Kelly allowed my father eventually to justify the dance costumes and the required exhibitions, but I don't think he was ever able to get over his resentment of being forced to be in the band instead of being allowed to play football. My grandmother's control over my father's activities in his early and teen years only reinforced the sexual issues which would plague my father all his life.

After graduating from high school, his parents sent my father for a post-graduate year at a military academy in another state. This was during World War II. Although the end of the war was in sight, my grandmother did not want my father to be drafted. After all, he might get hurt, or worse yet, killed. So, at the insistence of his mother my father dodged the draft. His failure to serve haunted my father the remainder of his life. All of his able-bodied peers had gone to war. It was yet another reflection on my father's manhood that he stayed behind attached to his mother's apron strings.

By the time the post-graduate year was over, so was the war. Perhaps there would have still been some hope for my father if his father had not died while my father was in college. My father had gone to the state university and was studying engineering. He would have made a good engineer. He had a mind for detail and rules were very important to him. Unfortunately, in the middle of his second year in college his father was diagnosed with a brain tumor. My father dropped out of school and returned home to be with his mother. Even though my father ultimately returned to college after his father died, his dreams of engineering were over. My grandmother wanted my father to get a banking degree and then to come home and work for her brother at the bank. There was no argument. My father changed majors, got his degree, moved back home with his mother, and went to work for his uncle.

As I mentioned, due to his relationship with his mother my father had huge sexual issues. To him women were either whores or virgins. There was nothing in between. My father did not date until college, and then very infrequently. The one young woman that I know he spent any time with after college was a family friend. He likely dated her for appearances. He told my brother and me that he did not date because he wasn't interested in spending money on a date. While I am sure there was some truth in my father's reluctance to spend money on a date – remember the mantra -- I believe now that his reluctance went much deeper than not wanting to spend money.

Let me elaborate.

I have mentioned earlier my father's temper. The word "temper" does not sufficiently describe the strength of the naked emotion that could emerge from my father's mouth at the drop of a hat. It was like living with an alcoholic. We never knew what would set him off. Whatever the trigger, filth and invective would erupt from my father's tongue, filling the room with intense black hatred. Then, as quickly as it started, the raging would stop.

One of those triggers was homosexuality. My father hated homosexuals. What we hate the most is also generally what we fear the most. Anger and fear are the same emotions presenting differently. One of my father's first cousins was a homosexual. Cousin Frank married and fathered a child while carrying on an affair with his homosexual lover. When Frank was "caught" the entire family was disgraced and Frank was banished to Atlanta. The only time we ever saw Frank after his banishment was at Christmas Day dinner when my father's extended family met at his Aunt and Uncle's home. I thought "Uncle" Frank was wonderful. He always told me and my mother how pretty we were, and he was great fun to be around. But he always sat in the living room with the women during those events, and never with the men who were smoking in the den. I guess there was a mini-banishment even in Frank's parents' home.

My mother's only brother was also a homosexual. I didn't even know my mother had a brother until I was in my teens and my mother and I ran into Charlie in the drug store. My mother started talking to this man without introducing me which was in and of itself unusual since it was a breach of Southern etiquette. After we walked off I asked my mother who the man was. When she told me he was her brother I was stunned. Why would my mother have kept this secret? What other secrets had she kept? When I asked her why we never saw him, she said he was the "black sheep" of the family and no one had anything to do with him. She refused to discuss him further.

I found out later that my mother's father had bailed out Charlie financially several times and then finally threw up his hands trying to deal with his son. Charlie was cut off from the family, and to my knowledge had very little contact with his siblings up until the time of his death. I have no idea what kind of life he lived, whether he had friends or lovers, whether he was happy or sad. I never saw him again after that one time. All I do know is that Charlie ended up living in a back room of one of the local funeral homes and drinking himself to death at the age of fifty. To my mother's credit, when Charlie was admitted to the hospital and was dying, she sat with him until the end. At least he did not die alone.

My mother was a secret-keeper. In addition to the secret she kept about her brother, my mother kept her first marriage a secret from me and my brother. I did not know until I was in high school that my mother had been married before she married my father. One day we were driving past the National Cemetery. It was Memorial Day and the cemetery was beautiful with rows and rows of small American flags waving in the light breeze over each small white grave marker. My mother turned to me and said she had something to tell me. In my wildest dreams I never imagined the words that she said next. "I was married before I met your father. My first husband is buried in that cemetery."

I was stunned. "Why did you not ever tell me this?" I asked her.

"Because," she replied, "your father did not want you to know."

My father did not want my brother or me to know about mother's first marriage because he was conflicted about my mother's sexual purity, or lack thereof. She was not a virgin when he married her since she was a widow. In my father's eyes, mother's lack of purity made her less valuable. He wasn't sure where she fit on his whore/virgin scale. I don't think there was a category for widows. Mother had not chosen to be a widow, but somehow the fact that another man had been with her first really bothered my father. It's not like it was a big secret among their friends. It just had to be a secret from me and my brother. My father's insistence on keeping this information from me even made me wonder at one point if I were really the child of my mother's first husband and my father had secretly adopted me. Why else, I thought, would it matter whether I knew about the first husband?

I have also wondered if my father was a repressed homosexual. He hated gay men with such an extraordinary vehemence. His face would turn red and he would almost literally foam at the mouth when talking about them. He stated on numerous occasions that "they" should all be killed. Maybe he worried that he was like his cousin Frank. For all I know, he and Frank may have had an encounter with each other. They were close in age to one another and had, of course, grown up together.

One of my more embarrassing moments with him was as an adult when my parents were visiting for the weekend and attended Sunday School with me. I was always afraid my father would say something inappropriate in public and on this particular occasion I had asked my mother to caution him about this in advance. She did, but as usual it did no good. In the middle of the class, and unrelated to anything being discussed, my father blurted out that AIDS was God's punishment for "queers," and that California should be dropped into the Pacific so most of "them" would be killed.

It would be hard for me to rank which phobia was more severe – my father's view about sex or his hatred of homosexuals. There is no doubt, however, where these phobias came from. They were the direct result of my father's relationship with his mother, exacerbated by the effects of his parents' marital dynamic. My father was emasculated by both of his parents. In fact, neither his father nor his mother perceived my father as a distinct and separate human being. To my grandfather, my father was a bargaining chip. My grandfather willingly sold my father to my grandmother in exchange for sexual freedom with his mistresses. To my grandmother, my father was a genderless toy. She dressed him the way she wanted, she refused to permit him to engage in regular male activities, and she required absolute obedience.

By the time he was a young adult, my father was consumed by sexual confusion and self-hatred. The older he became, the worse his demons grew. His anger was like a sleeping volcano. Hot, violent, and dangerous. Because he was never able to direct his anger where it belonged – toward his father or his mother – his anger erupted at inappropriate times and for seemingly ridiculous reasons.

In his own mind, my father was always Little Dickie. He never recovered from the effects of being discarded by his father, nor of being consumed by his mother. Even after his mother died, my father was unable to escape her. He had become who he was, and he was unable to change.

The Johnson Women

My mother was one of five daughters. Neither of her parents finished high school. Her father, the eldest of eleven children, had grown up in rural north Georgia. My grandfather's parents were killed when he was thirteen. My grandfather dropped out of school and became father and mother to his ten younger siblings. Eventually my grandfather became a successful salesman, and in his thirties married my grandmother when she was only fifteen years old. Nowadays that would get you arrested for statutory rape. Back then, particularly in the rural South, it was pretty much normal.

My grandmother had four children one after the other. A girl, a boy, another girl, and then my mother. My mother was a special child to my grandmother. Shortly before she became pregnant with my mother, my grandmother lost her oldest daughter to diphtheria. While my mother certainly could not replace her dead sister, my mother was a huge comfort to my grandmother, resulting in a close and special relationship between the two of them.

For most of my mother's growing-up years it was just mother, her older sister Janice and her brother Charlie. Then when my mother was fifteen, my grandmother gave birth to another daughter, Carol, and then seven years later, when my mother was twenty-two, my grandmother gave birth to her fifth daughter and last child, Peggy. My mother told me that my grandmother was so ignorant of her own body that during both of those late-life pregnancies she simply thought she "was going through the change."

There were only seven years of age difference between me and my mother's youngest sister, Peggy. It was both strange and fun growing up with an aunt who seemed much more like she should have been my sister. I have fond memories of sleepovers with my aunt when she was a teenager and I was five or six years old. Sometimes we would go to the Krystal for hamburgers and then to the movie theater for a show. To this day I love Krystal hamburgers – those tiny little meat patties on tiny, soft square buns with mustard, cheese, little onions, and a round dill pickle. Absolute heaven. On Saturday afternoons Aunt Peggy would let me watch American Bandstand with her and her girlfriends. We would dance in front of the black and white TV at my grandfather's house, singing our heads off to the music and twisting to the newest tunes. I also have some pretty creepy memories of my Aunt Peggy. She had long fingernails which she painted red. Sometimes she and her friends would delight in scaring me by acting like zombies. I can still see visions of my aunt coming after me with those long red nails while I screamed bloody murder and ran like Hell. In retrospect, I think maybe my Aunt Peggy saw me as some sort of exotic pet or live doll. No matter. She had a good time with me and most of the time I had a good time with her.

My grandmother Ruth was terrified of doctors, and as a result died at home of a heart attack which should not have killed her, when she was fifty-one and her youngest daughters were eight and fifteen years old. Even though she was experiencing severe chest pains she refused to go to the hospital. Finally, she let her husband call the doctor to come to the house, but by that time it was too late. She died in the downstairs front bedroom with my Aunt Peggy sitting right outside the door listening to the doctor pronounce her mother's death.

I have only one memory of Grandmother Ruth, and it is a dim one of sitting in her lap in a big, overstuffed chair in her living room. Most of my memories of that house and its inhabitants are of the sleepovers with my Aunt Peggy or going with my grandfather to his garden in the afternoons when he would return home from work. My grandfather remained a country boy at heart, and kept a huge garden for as long as he was able. I have no idea how large his lot was, but to the eyes of the young child that I was, it seemed to take forever to walk down to the garden. My Papa would have his cigarette in one hand and my hand in the other, and we would talk and examine each plant to see whether or not it was ready to be picked. I do not have any memory of actually picking any produce, although surely we did. All I remember is how good it felt to be with my grandfather in his garden in the late summer afternoons. There was nothing better.

My grandfather doted on the women in his family until his wife died. His wife's death changed him, and as a result, my mother and her older sister had very different growing-up experiences than did their two much younger sisters. Both my mother and her older sister Janice believed that they were special and that they were entitled to whatever they wanted. They weren't rude about it – they just expected to be treated as specially by other men as they were treated by their father. In her first husband, my mother found a man who loved her as completely as her father did and who treated her just as well. She was not so fortunate with her marriage to my father. And neither was her sister Janice in marrying her husband.

Mother and Aunt Janice married cruel and controlling men. I am really not sure how this came to pass. Cruel and controlling men would not seem likely to treat my mother and Aunt Janice in the doting and special way they had been treated by their father. Maybe my father and his clone, Aunt Janice's husband, were really Jekyll and Hyde characters. They acted one way and then after they captured and married their victims, they reverted to their true form. Whatever was the attraction for my mother and Aunt Janice, they both soon realized the error of their choices.

Both my mother and Aunt Janice tried to leave their respective husbands. In fact, Aunt Janice actually divorced her husband before she had any children. Just like my father had tricked my mother in their early marriage, Aunt Janice was tricked by her "ex" into remarrying him. Then, once Mother and Aunt Janice had children and tried to leave their respective marriages, it was too late. They were trapped and the price of leaving -- i.e., being "ruined socially" --was a price neither of them was willing to pay.

My father and Aunt Janice's husband were two peas in a pod. Both were self-righteous, controlling, chauvinistic egotists. Neither liked the other, most likely because they saw the reflection of themselves in each other and did not like what they saw. Both ruled their families with an iron fist and punished the dissenters unmercifully. Once, when my mother criticized the aesthetics of a home my uncle had built, he forbade Aunt Janice and my cousins from speaking to my mother or to any of the rest of us. Aunt Janice was so afraid of her husband that she obeyed him, and for a period of ten or more years she did not have any contact with my mother. Then, the Thanksgiving of my first semester in college, Aunt Janice invited all of us to their house for Thanksgiving dinner. Nothing was ever said. No apology. No discussion. No explanation. It was as if the past ten years had never happened. My mother and Aunt Janice were just happy to have permission to be able to talk to each other again.

The lives of the two younger Johnson women were greatly affected by the death of their mother and their father's resulting inability to deal with the demands of raising eight- and fifteen-year-old girls. I guess raising his ten siblings had taken all my grandfather could give as a parent. My grandfather thrust the parenting role on the shoulders of his fifteen-year-old daughter Carol and never looked back. He loved his daughters until the day he died, but with the death of his wife he absconded from all parental duties.

The youngest daughter, my Aunt Peggy, never recovered from her mother's death. At the age of eight my Aunt Peggy desperately needed a mother. It was all her older sister Carol could do at age fifteen to manage the house. She simply could not be a mother to her younger sister. Neither my mother nor Aunt Janice offered any assistance to their younger siblings. In fact, my Aunt Carol recounts with bitterness my mother coming into the house , running her fingers over the furniture and stating with disdain, "Dust." The deepest conversation either my mother or Aunt Janice ever had with my Aunt Carol was before Aunt Carol married, when they warned her that all men wanted was sex and that Aunt Carol's new husband would climb on top of her and say "Hail Marys" while satisfying himself (he was Catholic). What a thinly veiled commentary on their own marital experiences.

The Johnson girls were, as are all of us, a result of their environment in their formative years. Fear of social opprobrium resulted in my mother and her older sister being unable to leave marriages to abusive and controlling men. My Aunt Peggy developed serious mental illness and has lived her entire life as an abandoned child, wanting others to take care of her. My Aunt Carol undertook the role of caretaker for years before finally being able to take the steps necessary to care for herself. Of the four surviving girls, only my Aunt Carol was able to choose the difficult road of introspection and as a result has been able to have a happy and fulfilling life.

I wish my mother could have made that choice. Instead she chose my father – a man who did not hold my mother in any particular esteem, who had no intention of doting on her as her father and first husband had done, and who expected my mother to do exactly as he told her, without argument or complaint. Less than two years into her marriage to my father, my mother was a broken woman.

The Son

My father was not prepared to have a daughter as a first child. In fact, he refused to even consider any female names while my mother was pregnant because having a daughter was not in his plan. So, when I was born there was no name picked out for me. In order to have something to put on the birth certificate, my parents gave me their middle names. Fortunately for me, they were nice names.

When I was four years old my brother Dan was born. As expected, my father was elated. The reason for my father's elation was simple. In a son my father saw a chance for his own salvation. My brother was the vehicle through which my father could live his life over. And so it began.

My brother was named after my father's father. By the time my brother was born my father had engaged in revisionist history, and now had his own father on a pedestal fifty feet high. My grandfather was no longer the philandering playboy. To the contrary, he was the finest man who had ever lived and the person against whom my father measured all other men. Carrying his grandfather's name was the first of many strikes against my brother. There was no way he could ever measure up to someone who was perfect, even if perfect only in fiction.

Since my father had been forbidden from playing sports, my father decided that my brother would be an athlete. Step one in my father's second chance at life. When Dan was three years old my father began requiring my brother to throw a baseball and a small football with him on a daily basis. It did not matter that my brother was not interested in playing catch. My father demanded it. In addition to mandatory throwing practice, my brother was required to watch baseball and football games on television. Dan would cry and cry over this. He just wanted to play outside. My father would have none of it.

When my brother was in elementary school he played flag football in a citywide league. In flag football, instead of tackling the opponent, the player pulls off his opponent's flag which is worn on a belt around the waist. I don't know if flag football is played any longer, but it was a big deal with the elementary school crowd in the 1960s. My brother played flag football for three years, from the fourth grade through the sixth grade. Of course my father was the coach. And of course my brother was the quarterback.

My father refused to put any boy in the game unless the boy could "perform." My father did not believe in letting every child have an opportunity to play. My father had two goals as coach: to make my brother look good, and to win. If you couldn't contribute to those goals, you didn't play. If you made a mistake on the field, you were immediately pulled out of the game and berated on the sidelines. It is really amazing that my father was allowed to get away with this behavior and coach the team for three years. I remember there were parents who were really upset about the exclusion of their sons from being allowed to play in the games, as well as how my father treated the players, but they either could not or would not make my father change his rules.

Every activity in our house revolved around my brother's sports. On Saturdays we went to flag football games or to basketball games, depending on the season. Once spring rolled around, we were at the Little League park until late into the evening. In the summer, we were there several times a week. The absolute last thing I was interested in was attending my brother's sports events. My feelings were irrelevant. Like all of my father's rules, there was no room for argument. Attendance at my brother's sporting events was mandatory.

My father's hard work paid off. Dan became a stellar athlete. My brother also became arrogant, rigid and -- like our father -- afflicted with a severe case of Right's Disease. To start, my brother believed all the bullshit he had heard from our father over the years. Specifically, my brother believed he was better than anyone else and that the rules did not apply to him. There was no disputing Dan's athletic prowess. But with great gifts should also come great humility. My brother's attitude toward his peers was so vain that he was blackballed by them from every club and society in his school. My father's response to all of this was that "they" were jealous of my brother's abilities. Neither my father nor my brother ever considered that my brother might have had a role in what happened. This question never crossed their minds.

By the time Dan was a senior in high school his picture had been plastered all over the local newspaper sports section twenty or thirty times. I am not talking about a small picture. I am talking major -- the entire page big. He had been selected for every VIP team in every sport. My father cut out each article and had it framed. The walls in the den became a visual shrine to Dan's athletic accomplishments. His senior year in high school my brother passed for over 1000 yards. Two of his receivers went on to play college football and then professional football. The difference between the receivers and my brother was not talent. It was height. The receivers were over six feet tall. Dan was five foot ten, maybe.

True to form, my father ignored reality, in this case my brother's physical limitations. My father told my brother he was good enough to play quarterback at an SEC school, and my brother believed him. For those of you who are sports illiterates, the SEC was, and is, the Southeastern Conference. All of the big Southern schools are members of the SEC – Alabama, Tennessee, Georgia to name a few. My father considered the SEC to have the best football teams in the country. Of course, not a single SEC school was interested in my brother. He was never going to be tall enough to play in that league. But other schools were interested in my brother. One small college offered him a full athletic scholarship plus a car -- the car being an under the table gift, of course, because giving my brother a car as a recruitment incentive violated about a thousand NCAA rules. Another small college actively recruited my brother as well as one of my brother's receivers. Those two would have made an unbeatable combination. My father refused to even consider that college for my brother because it did not offer athletic scholarships. My father said he wasn't paying for my brother to play football when colleges should be paying Dan to play for them. My brother's third opportunity was priceless. He was given the option of an appointment to West Point. He dismissed that offer out of hand.

Instead, my brother went to the University of Alabama and tried out for the football team. He failed. No one was surprised except my father and my brother.

Many people have a defining moment when something happens and their life is forever changed. Sometimes it is for the better, sometimes just the opposite. For others, there is a turning point when the person makes a cognitive choice for one path or another. I think both were true for Dan. My brother's sense of self was completely dependent on being a star athlete. When his ability to function as an athlete was lost to him after high school, my brother lost his center and source of reference for the world around him.

Dan found himself at the turning point. One road was unknown. Taking that unknown road would require my brother to take a huge psychological risk. My father had directed my brother's life for eighteen years, and had made every major decision for him. Choosing the unknown road meant self-actualization and responsibility for his own decisions. It meant the possibility of failure. It meant an unknown future. It was a terrifying prospect for my brother.

The other road was much safer. The safe road meant that my brother would not have to take risks. He could continue to rely on our father. He would not have to accept responsibility for his actions. He knew his father would never let him fail.

Did my brother recognize his defining moment when it occurred? Did he weigh the pros and cons of choosing one road over the other? Of course not. None of us have that clarity of vision while we are in the moment. It is only in retrospect, sometimes after the passage of many years, that we are able to see and understand the moment and the choice. And some of us, like my brother, never see or understand.

The Daughter

My father never really knew what to do with me. As I mentioned earlier, he was not prepared to have a daughter as his first-born. Certainly there was not much I could offer my father in the way of self-fulfillment. No opportunity to live his life over like he eventually had with my brother. My father's only concern for me, and I heard it ad nauseam, was that I marry a rich man. When I wasn't hearing that from my father I heard it from my mother. Marrying well was a woman's highest goal. I guess that was the female equivalent of being a star athlete.

I was largely ignored by my father so long as I did what he told me to do, followed his rules, and did not "back talk." Back talking was a particularly heinous crime. Two examples come immediately to mind. The first was when I was twelve or thirteen. All four of us – mother, father, brother and myself – were eating supper at the kitchen table. Everyone had an assigned seat, and mine was between my father and my brother. I don't remember what the topic was or what I said, but whatever it was, it triggered my father's rage. Out of no where his right hand whipped across my face, knocking me out of my chair and onto the floor. "Don't you ever speak to me like that!" he roared. My mother never said a word nor did she make any attempt to console me. Had she taken my side he would probably have hit her too.

The second event of note happened between my first and second year of college. My boyfriend and I were sitting in the den talking. My father came into the room and said something to me. I don't remember if he asked me to do something, or if he was asking me a question. Whatever I said in response infuriated him. He grabbed me off the sofa and started dragging me down the hallway, hitting me with his other hand and yelling at me. All of this in front of my boyfriend who sat in stunned silence. I was mortified and humiliated. After it was all over, my father acted like nothing had happened.

My father saw nothing wrong with beating the crap out of me. My brother got off light in this regard. His male status and his athletic standing afforded him quite a bit of protection. Also, my brother was never held to the same academic standard to which I was held by my father. Consequently, physical attacks on my brother were few and far between.

Not so with me. My father's thick wooden fraternity paddle was the instrument of abuse. If I brought home a B on a report card I got the paddle. If I broke a rule I got the paddle. If I talked back I got the paddle. There was never a discussion of the infraction and an opportunity to improve. It was always the paddle.

My father would send me to his home office to get the paddle, which was prominently displayed on the office wall along with my father's other important memorabilia, including the revered KKK picture. When I brought the paddle back to my father he would make me bend over and grab my ankles. He would hit me so hard that the force of the impact would move me three or four feet across the room. If I started crying before the paddling, my father would start laughing. He was a regular sadist. My father continued this form of punishment until I was well past puberty. At that point the paddling had developed a sexual overtone. Having to bend over with my ass in my father's face made me feel somehow exposed, even though I was fully clothed. That feeling was worse than the pain from the paddle.

My mother saw it all, but she never intervened.

I had my heart set on attending Middlebury College. It was the premier language school at the collegiate level. By the time I was a senior in high school I was so proficient in French that I dreamed in the language. Middlebury College would permit me to live in a French-speaking dorm and to take a year abroad. My father would have none of it. His reason? The school was above the Mason-Dixon line, I would marry a Yankee, and he would never see me again. My only "choice" was to go to the state University. He told me that the state University had been good enough for him and it would be good enough for me.

My instructions upon entering college were made abundantly clear to me. I was to pledge either Chi Omega Sorority or Delta Delta Delta Sorority because those were the most prestigious sororities. Nothing else was acceptable. In what was to be my first step in rebellion, I pledged a different sorority. While this may not seem like a rebellious act to most people, it was a big step for me. My father was not happy with my choice, but since a doctor's daughter (read: "social status") from my high school had also pledged that sorority, my father decided that the sorority was acceptable.

I was miserable. The first semester I went to the classes I liked and skipped the rest. I had two A's and three F's. I hid the report card from my father. I went back in January and lasted two months. I had gained forty-five pounds and was in a deep depression. I dropped out of school and went home.

It was clear to anyone who had eyes that something was badly wrong with me. My father's only comment to me was, "You are as fat as a pig." My father knew a man who owned a fitness gym. He took me down to the gym, introduced me to the owner, and said, "I want you to get that weight off of her." I can't adequately express how bad I felt about myself at that point. I know I felt less than worthless. All I wanted to do was crawl into a cave and cry.

My father told me I was to go to the gym every day. I disobeyed him. Each day I would dress in exercise clothes and drive to a small park. There I would spend the next hour or so reading a book. My mother never questioned my lack of sweaty clothes when I would return home, nor did she say anything about it to my father. Maybe remaining silent was her own way of disobeying my father.

I don't know how I finally got to a medical doctor for an examination. Thank God I did. I was diagnosed with a severely underfunctioning thyroid. The weight gain and the depression were classic symptoms. My father's response to my diagnosis was to accuse me of taking drugs. He said I must have done something to cause my thyroid gland to malfunction. As always, it had to be my fault.

I wish I could tell you that the events of my first year of college were the defining moment that allowed me to see my father for what he was, and to be able to move beyond him. Such was not the case. I returned to school, obtained undergraduate and post- graduate degrees, and then married well. Unfortunately, I traded an abusive father for an abusive husband. And I paid dearly for that choice.

The Iron Fist

The method my father used to combat his insecurity was to exercise complete control over my mother, my brother, and myself. This pathological need manifested itself differently with each of us. With my mother, control took the form of verbal abuse. With me, control took the form of physical abuse and intimidation. With my brother, control took the form of money.

My father figuratively beat my mother into such submission in their marriage that she lost her voice. She never corrected him. She never intervened when he was raging at or hitting me. She simply did not talk. I don't mean that she actually became mute. My father simply wore out my mother to such an extent that she lost the will or energy to fight him. They lived lonely and separate lives in the same space for almost fifty-five years. In many ways she simply faded away.

My father said terrible things to my mother. I can't count the times he told her she was stupid or that she needed "to just shut up." One time he told her, in front of me, my husband, and my youngest child, that he wasn't interested in her because she had "just dried up." I was so embarrassed for my mother. The sexual content of that remark did not escape me. My mother made no response. She just hung her head and sat in silence. The fact is, my father did not pay one bit of attention to my mother until she had her second stroke, and then he was kind and attentive to her only because it suited his purposes, and only in public. He continued to berate and belittle her in private until the day he died.

My parents had no social life. They never went out as a couple. The most likely reason for this was that no one could stand to be around my father for any period of time. My father's favorite subject was himself and he dominated every conversation, extolling his personal merits, all of which were imagined. According to my father, he was responsible for the success of at least half of the local businessmen because he "had given them their start" by giving them a bank loan at some point in the distant past. I could have put my father in front of a wall and he would have talked to the wall for hours. He did not need an audience. He just needed to hear himself talk about himself.

I lived in absolute fear of my father. A child who grows up with an active alcoholic expends a huge amount of energy trying to manage the environment so the alcoholic won't drink. The child believes that there must be something he or she can do to prevent that first drink and the terrible results that flow from it. I did the same thing. Because I never knew what might trigger one of my father's rages, I tried to be perfect. I made good grades. I played intramural sports (which did not count because they were girl sports). I was selected for prestigious clubs and was named an editor of my high school yearbook. I dated the right boys. I did not drink, I never received a demerit my entire six years in a strict private girls' school, and I never got in trouble. It did not matter. It was never enough. There was always some infraction. The rages continued and I was beaten with that paddle until I graduated from high school.

I have written of my father's control over my brother's early years relative to sports. Once my brother accepted his role as athlete, the need for my father to exert control over my brother's actions significantly diminished. This changed dramatically when my brother was in his second year of college. After my brother failed to make the football team at the University of Alabama, he transferred to the University of Kentucky. My brother had never paid much attention to excelling in the classroom. I guess he thought that the pro football career my father had promised him would provide plenty of money. He had not studied in high school and his attitude toward studying did not change in college. My brother proceeded to party, use and sell drugs, and to get his girlfriend pregnant. At one point my brother almost got himself killed selling drugs because he owed his supplier money. Although my father may have bailed out my brother on previous occasions, that was the first one I knew about. Instead of exacting punishment from my brother for selling drugs, my father simply paid off the debt. It was as if it never happened.

The partying ended with the girlfriend's pregnancy. Actually there were two pregnancies. The first pregnancy "disappeared". Unfortunately, religious guilt got the better of her, and she deliberately got pregnant again, this time insisting that my brother marry her. Maybe that was supposed to provide penance for the disappearing pregnancy.

To say that my father was pissed would be a gross understatement. Among my father's numerous rules was one which stood above the rest. My brother and I had been ordered not to date "niggers, Jews or Catholics." The girlfriend was Catholic. I don't know which infuriated my father more – the fact that my brother had gotten this girl pregnant or the fact that she was Catholic.

My father was absolutely rabid about Catholics. I never understood why. He just was. I have several Catholic stories, but the one I remember most involved my favorite aunt. Aunt Carol had married a very nice Catholic man when I was in elementary school. When my Aunt Carol and her husband were in town they stayed with her in-laws, an absolutely delightful couple who had immigrated from Spain in their early years. Although I was invited many times to dinner with my aunt, my father refused to let me go for the sole reason that the family was Catholic. I guess he thought they would try to convert me at the dinner table.

Her Catholicism notwithstanding, my brother married his girlfriend, dropped out of college and, at my father's insistence, moved back to Chattanooga. Thus began a malignantly symbiotic relationship between my father and brother which made their previous relationship appear almost benign. From the time my brother married his wife until the day my father died, my brother was financially supported either completely or partially by my father. My father could not permit his own father's namesake to fail. For almost thirty years, my father refused to let Dan suffer the consequences of his actions and bad choices, and instead blamed everything on my brother's wife. My sister-in-law, of course, never had a chance. My father and mother demonized her to such a great extent that my brother eventually believed everything that was said about his wife.

My father offered my brother a safety net. Dan saw and chose the safe road. Little did my brother know that his choice would lead to his total emasculation and slow descent into insanity.

Married Well

I was sent to a private girls' school for seventh through twelfth grades. The school was quite strict. We wore uniforms with saddle oxfords and white socks. No makeup or jewelry was allowed other than watches, rings, and religious medals. The school acquiesced to pierced ears in the late sixties, but we could only wear small gold or silver ball earrings. Although not religiously affiliated with any denomination, the founders of the school had been staunch Presbyterians and believed that Bible learning was a worthy goal. To that end, each day started with mandatory chapel, where students would learn another verse or two of selected scripture until each grade could stand in chapel and recite from memory entire chapters from the Bible.

This school had been founded in the early 1900s to provide a cloistered education for the young women of Chattanooga's elite. While the school provided an excellent academic experience, it was slow to recognize the changing role of women. For example, in the 1960s when I was a student, neither typing nor home economics was taught. Typing was needed only if one were going to actually have a job. Home economics was for those who could not afford servants. No girl attending this school was ever expected to find herself working or without domestic help.

In my father's eyes this was the dream school for me. I was enrolled before I was a year old. For you see, attending this school was step one in marrying well.

There were two boys' schools in Chattanooga. As mentioned earlier, my father had attended one of them for his high school years, and it was as a student at that same school that my brother became a high school athletic legend. During my high school years my father forbade me from dating any boy who did not attend one of the local boys' schools. My father instructed me I was to associate only with my peers, who, according to my father, did not attend public school.

Actually, my peers did attend public school, and on a socioeconomic level that is where I should have gone to school. Unfortunately, my father placed me in an elite private school without the tools needed to succeed. I was handicapped from the start.

Most of the girls who were in school with me were from very wealthy families. Their homes were huge and lovely. Some of them actually had servants. I will never forget my first experience of being served dinner by a friend's family cook. I was spending the night with this friend at her family's summer home, which was actually a very nice large cottage on the back of Signal Mountain in an area known by the name of "Summer Town." Summer Town was a wooded and secluded area where, in the early 1900s, wealthy Chattanoogans kept summer homes. It was cooler on the mountain and in an era without air conditioning, that was an important consideration in a Southern summer. Over the years, and even with the advent of air conditioning, many of Chattanooga's wealthy families maintained a summer or weekend home in Summer Town.

Even though we were in my friend's more casual home, we were seated for dinner, of course, in the dining room. My friend's mother pressed a buzzer under the table and a servant began bringing in the meal, serving each of us at our place. I must have made some terrible gaffe that evening at dinner, because the next day at lunch, when fried chicken was served, my friend's mother told the cook to take away the knives so we wouldn't have to use them and could eat the chicken with our fingers. I was embarrassed. I never knew anyone who ate fried chicken with a knife and fork, and I knew that my friend's mother knew that about me. I was not sure why that made me feel badly, but it did. I felt I had been given an opportunity to pass some sort of unspoken but important test and that I had failed. Although my friend remained cordial at school, I was never again invited to her home.

Besides having lovely, well-appointed homes and memberships in the local country clubs, my classmates also went to expensive camps in the summer, and to the beaches or the Caribbean in the winter. On the weekends, when we did not have to wear our school uniforms, my school friends wore Villager or Lady Bug outfits with Capezio slippers.

My life was a stark contrast. We lived in a small house which was meagerly furnished. My mother had an eye for design, but my father refused to let her spend money decorating the house. When all of my friends went to summer camp, my father denied me that opportunity, telling me that camp was a waste of money. We never took a vacation. My father thought that vacations were a frivolity, and that one's time was better spent working instead of wasting money on travel. It goes without saying that my weekend attire was certainly not name brand. By the time I was fourteen or fifteen I knew that being pretty and smart was not enough to be accepted by the majority of the people in my school. I lacked the most important criteria: money, and what it could buy.

My senior year in high school I got my first painful lesson in what money could buy. Every spring the school would celebrate May Day. The members of the senior class would secretly nominate five candidates from the senior class for May Queen and Maid of Honor. Then, the entire school would vote for the winner.

More than anything I wanted to be selected as the Maid of Honor. It was my only goal for five years. My senior year I was one of the five girls nominated by my classmates for Maid of Honor. When the school voted, the selection was narrowed to a run-off between me and another girl. When she won I was crushed. It would have been hard enough had she won fair and square. But she had not. A teacher who meant well, and who saw how devastated I continued to be over the loss even months after the election, told me that I had garnered the most votes from the student body but that "the faculty" had selected the other girl because her parents had been large financial contributors to the school and were socially prominent. I guess the teacher thought it would make me feel better to know what had really occurred. It did not.

Had my father not imprinted on my mind the importance of position and money, maybe I would have eventually shrugged off the Maid of Honor incident. But imprinting is hard to overcome. The message that was incorporated into my psyche as a result of that undeserved loss was that money is power. I decided then that my father was right. Money and position were all that mattered. By the time I went to college I had determined to marry well. Money was going to give me what I so desperately craved. I was finally going to be good enough.

My chance to marry well came when I was in my mid-twenties. The man who became my first husband was from a wealthy family who owned lucrative businesses in several states. They also owned race horses, one of which had won the Kentucky Derby. The women shopped in New York and the family spent the winter months in the Caribbean. My father was ecstatic when we announced our engagement.

They say we pick our parent of the opposite sex when we select our mate. I don't know if that is completely true or not. The only similarities I ever saw between my father and my first husband – and I never recognized these traits until years later -- were that they both loved money and they both were abusers of women. Of course, both of those similarities were deadly.

My first marriage was probably doomed from the start. I married my first husband even though he had beaten me on two occasions when we were dating. I knew that physical abuse was wrong, but the lure of marrying well and the life I thought it would give me was too great. Amazingly, he never hit me after we were married. He simply switched his physical abuse to that of the verbal and emotional sort. Frankly, I think it was worse than being hit.

My first husband Sam was too busy worrying about how badly his life had turned out to be concerned about our marriage. His family had sold their businesses and my husband had no idea what he was going to do to earn a living. He was bitter about the sale of the businesses, and would complain endlessly about how unfair it was that his livelihood had been taken away from him. My husband had intended to live the way his father had lived, going to the office each morning and playing golf each afternoon. Someone else would do the hard work of running the businesses. He would just spend the profits. My husband ended up being a stockbroker and hated every minute of it. I think he thought sales was somehow demeaning. It was difficult for him and he was not very good at it.

In the meantime, our marriage went from bad to worse. When I got pregnant with our first child I knew he would be angry, so I told him in a parking lot after work. In a fit of anger he threw his sunglasses to the ground, screaming at me that I had ruined his life because by getting pregnant I had taken away from him the one thing that mattered to him – traveling. I thought that was a really odd comment then, and I still think so now, although I think I have a better understanding now of what he meant. Sam did not want responsibility. He had seen his father live an entire life of leisure without being responsible, and that was what he had expected in his own life. When the businesses were sold, and the expectation of financial freedom was no longer a possibility, much less a reality, my husband had difficulty accepting life on life's terms. Having a child brought that reality much closer than Sam wanted it to be. I really do think he thought his life was over.

My response to the parking lot tirade was to leave the marriage. Sam begged me to return. He swore he didn't mean anything he had said. If only I would come back he would never act like that again. I believed him. I went back. The next two years were hell. I tried everything to make the marriage work. I quit work and became a housewife like all of his friends' wives. I went back to work because Sam was angry about having to work while I did not. Finally, I got pregnant again, this time because Sam wanted a son. I did everything you read about to try to make him happy. None of it worked.

I am sure you have heard that joke about the man who wakes up one morning and finds sleeping in the bed next to him is the ugliest woman he has ever seen. He is horrified to realize that his arm is under the woman's head. The woman is so ugly that the man chews off his arm so he can escape without waking her up. Men think this joke is hilarious, but it is really a story about self-preservation. And I understand the psychology of it completely. When my second child was less than two years old I reached the limit of my ability to suffer the emotional abuse meted out by my husband. In an act of absolute self-preservation, I left him. I wish I had done it better than I did. I left Sam for another man.

I never thought I would lose my children. My lawyer, whom I had selected based on his social status rather than any expertise in divorce law, had assured me that I had nothing to worry about in that regard. My lawyer did not understand my husband, his family, or their power -- and neither did I. Just as my mother and I had been my father's possessions, so too did Sam consider the children to be his possessions. He also considered them the only way in which he could really hurt me. And he was right.

The judge who heard the divorce had been a close friend of Sam's grandfather. They had been deacons together at the First Baptist Church, although I did not know that until much later. The judge awarded joint custody in name only. The children and I had moved to Washington DC for my job as a federal prosecutor during the pendency of the divorce. The judge ruled that Washington DC was an unfit place to raise children, and decreed that my children would live with their father in Tennessee. I could see them for six weeks in the summer and alternating holidays.

I began crying in the courtroom. The price of my self-preservation was much more than just an arm.

Don't Worry, Daddy Is Here

My brother Dan dropped out of college after he got married. He was either nineteen or twenty. He tried to go to night classes after his son was born, but his wife threw fits because she said she didn't – in her words "want to be stuck with the baby all the time." Thus was set the tone of their marriage. A year after baby one was born, baby two arrived. During this period of time neither my brother nor his wife held any particular type of gainful employment. Why bother? My father was supporting them. I imagine my father paid the obstetrician's bills as well as the rent, the groceries, the insurance, and the car notes.

My brother could not hold a job for more than a few years without getting fired. In his mind, he was still the star athlete. Dan believed he knew more than his bosses, and he was still arrogant. People could not stand to work with him. Every time Dan lost a job, my father would make excuses for him. The loss of a job could never be my brother's fault. My father would then start paying my brother's bills and supporting his family until my brother was able to find another job.

After several job losses, my father decided to set my brother up in a business of his own. There is no telling how much money my father put into that endeavor. Of course, true to form, Dan spent what income came into the company and ignored paying the company bills and taxes. When Dan was pursued by the IRS for not paying employee withholding taxes, and was in danger of having a tax lien placed on his house, guess who paid off the IRS? That's right. My father.

Now, wait a minute, you say. How could my brother have afforded a house? Surely by now you have figured that one out. My father bought my brother a house in a prestigious neighborhood and paid for his membership in the Country Club. After all, status must be pursued at all costs. My father paid the mortgage on my brother's house and then deeded it to him free and clear. After a few years, Dan put a new mortgage on his house so he could have "spending money." When Dan could not make the payments, my father paid off the mortgage a second time so that my brother's house was free and clear once again. Less than ten years later, my brother had three new mortgages on the house, four children, and a failed business.

My brother's business failed even with an investor other than my father. Dan had a friend who had attended school with him. The friend had plenty of money and, according to my brother, decided to invest in my brother's business. Even after the business failed, the man continued to give my brother substantial money on a regular monthly basis. This went on for several years. My mother, who rarely ventured an opinion, told me more than once that she thought that something was wrong with the relationship between Dan and this man. The man's personal situation disturbed her. He was in his forties, had never married, and lived with his parents. She even asked me at one point if I thought my brother was engaged in an "improper" relationship with the man. I did, but I did not tell her so. There was only so much information my mother really wanted to have.

There were long periods of time when Dan was in his thirties and forties when he was unemployed. When these periods occurred, my father paid the private school tuition for my brother's children – for of course they could not attend a public school – and put food on my brother's table so the children would have food to eat. My brother saw nothing wrong with this. And he made no real effort to find gainful employment. By the time he was in his late forties, Dan was no longer employable in Chattanooga. The business community had his number.

The last job my brother had came about when he was forty-eight or forty-nine. Of course that did not work out either. Instead of devoting himself to his employer's business, Dan spent half his time pursuing a fantasy business deal that he claimed was going to make him millions. My brother saw the ages of fifty and fifty-one come and go without employment of any sort. He quit looking for work, secluded himself in his house, and waited to become a millionaire.

This time, however, my father was not around to save my brother. My father was dead, and the fountain of money had run dry. The last money my brother got from my father was on the day my father died. My father died of cancer. When he was in the last stages of the disease, I moved my father and my mother into a guest cottage at my home. Two days before he died Lawrence and I made the decision to move my father to a residential hospice so that his pain could be controlled sufficiently and he would not suffer. My mother was with my father when he died. After my mother had a chance to say her goodbyes at the hospice, my brother took her and my mother's companion back to the cottage while Lawrence and I attended to the remaining details at the hospice. When my brother got to the cottage he immediately began rifling through my father's possessions, looking for my father's wallet. Dan took every dollar out of my father's wallet – the huge sum of eighty-seven dollars -- told my mother he needed the cash to get back to Chattanooga, and walked out.

My brother stole my father's money from his wallet before my father's body was cold. You can't get any lower than that.

Descent Into Darkness

Without a doubt, losing my children was the worst thing that ever happened to me. In 1984 when this happened, I had never heard of a woman losing custody of her children in a divorce. Even though Sam had counter-sued for sole custody, my attorney told me I had nothing to worry about. He told me I was a good mother, and that because I was a good mother I could have been a hooker in a ghetto and not have lost my children.

During the seven years I was married to Sam I was both mother and father to my children, as well as a parent to my husband . When I had my first child I was working full time. I was given six weeks of maternity leave, generous at the time, and then returned to work full time. Of course my daughter was not sleeping through the night when she was six weeks old. I would be up at 5:00 a.m. to feed her, and to get myself ready for work and out the door. When I got home from work I would cook supper, bathe and feed my daughter, do laundry, get her in bed at 7:00 p.m., take my shower, sleep for a few hours, then get up for her 11:00 p.m. feeding, back to bed, and then up again at 3:00 a.m. or so for another feeding, then back to bed for an hour or so, then start it all over again. I did not have to worry about losing my pregnancy weight. I was eating like a deck hand and burning off weight faster than I could fuel my body.

Did Sam help? You must be kidding. He came home from work, dropped his suit on the bedroom floor for me to pick up, got a beer, and plopped himself down on the sofa to watch TV. He expected me to serve him his supper on a tray in front of the TV. He never washed a dish. He never ran a load of laundry. He never cooked a meal. He never gave our daughter a bottle or helped to bathe her. And it goes without saying that he never changed a diaper. On Saturdays and Sundays he went to the club to play golf. After all, this child was the result of the pregnancy that he said had ruined his life.

Sam had nothing to do with our daughter or with me. He was not interested.

When our son was born, Sam seemed glad to have a boy. The dynasty was continued and my son was a "IV." However, being glad to have a namesake did not change my husband's attitude toward childcare. Once again, he never lifted a hand.

Our marriage had developed serious trouble in the months before I got pregnant with our son. One of the underlying causes of this conflict was Sam's attitude about my employment. I held a professional degree and had a position in a prestigious law firm. My husband wanted my extra income, but my position made him feel inferior. After all, he attended seven colleges in as many years before he attained a history degree. Although older than me, he graduated from college one semester before I graduated from law school. So, in an attempt to address this issue, I "retired" to be a stay-at-home mother with our daughter. During this time I became pregnant with our son. However, when our son was five months old, Sam insisted I return to work. I think the real reason for his insistence in this regard was more than wanting extra income. My husband hated having to work, and I believe that he decided if he had to work, then so did I.

When I went back to work I did not return to private practice. The demands of private practice were simply too demanding for a mother who was for all intents and purposes a single mother with two small children. I was fortunate to find a government position with more regular hours. I also found my future husband, Lawrence.

I wrote earlier that I wish I had left my first marriage under different circumstances, but I realize in retrospect that I did not have the ability to walk out by myself and would never had been able to leave of my own accord. The emotional abuse I had suffered first at the hands of my father and then at the hands of my first husband had taken away from me any sense of self-worth and beaten me into an accepting submission. Even though I was a successful professional, I did not feel "successful" as a person. I needed a rescuer. And I found one.

My biggest mistake in my divorce was expecting Sam to act like an adult. Our marriage was long over, neither one of us liked, much less loved, the other, and Sam did not want to be a parent. I did not ask for alimony. I thought that was wrong since I could support myself. All I wanted was my children and financial support for them. I should have gone for Sam's money. That was my leverage. Sam would have done anything to protect his money, and the children would not have been an issue.

My second mistake was in not understanding the effect on Sam's psyche of my asking for a divorce. Sam had grown up in an alcoholic family. His father was such a bad alcoholic that he would pass out at the dinner table. Sam's mother was a huge enabler. She ignored her husband's alcoholism because she did not want to lose her lifestyle. When Sam was a child his parents traveled extensively, leaving him and his sister to be raised by a housekeeper for extended periods of time. When he was fourteen he was shipped off to boarding school.

Children of alcoholics have an overriding sense of abandonment, and unless they address that issue through therapy, every relationship they have will suffer. Given the circumstances of his upbringing, Sam had suffered a double whammy. In addition to the abandonment issues brought up by the psychological effects of an alcoholic household, Sam suffered from the abandonment issues based on his parents' actual physical abandonment of him while they lived their own extravagant lifestyle. When I walked out of our marriage, and took my children with me, all Sam felt was that he was once again being abandoned. All of the anger and pain Sam had experienced since childhood became directed at me. And it came at me with a vengeance. He told me at one point that "no one in their right mind would want to be married to a bitch like you, but I will never let you have a divorce." Of course he changed his mind about the divorce, but not about anything else.

Although I could never prove it, I feel certain that Sam's family connections with the judge sealed my fate and that of my children. I never denied my extramarital relationship. The state's Supreme Court had ruled in several prior cases that adultery was not a sufficient reason for taking custody of small children away from their mother. Because this was the law, my lawyer assured me that I would be awarded custody of my children. The judge had a different idea. Although he awarded joint legal custody to both Sam and me, the judge awarded actual physical custody of the children to Sam. The judge rendered a decision which found that Washington DC – where the children and I were living -- was an unfit place to raise children. Ergo, since I was living in Washington DC, the children were to live with their father. My daughter was four and a half. My son was two years old. The judge found his own way to punish me, and he got away with it.

The children were to return to DC with me after the divorce for a period of three months. After that they were to live with their father. My daughter knew what was happening. The child psychologist who testified for me during the divorce trial told the judge that my daughter would be devastated if she were separated from me. She was right. My daughter asked me time and time again why she couldn't stay with me and just let her brother live with her father. The day Sam came to pick up the children to return with him to Tennessee my daughter became hysterical, screaming and clinging to me like a drowning man clings to a piece of floating debris. My daughter had to be physically pried off of me by her father. My daughter fought and screamed the entire way to her father's car. It nearly killed both of us.

It has been twenty-three years since that day, and as I write this the pain is as fresh and as powerful as it was on that very day. Even though I made the correct choice for self-preservation, the manner in which I implemented that choice had unintended and disastrous effects for my children.

Soon after my divorce I married my rescuer, became pregnant, and had another child. During the eighteen months that we remained in Washington, I called my two older children three times a week. I wanted to keep that contact constant and regular. After our divorce Sam started dating a wealthy woman from a prominent Knoxville family. Once when I called the children, this woman answered the phone. When I asked to speak to my children, she said, "Why don't you give up?" and slammed down the phone, cutting off my call. On more than one occasion I would call to be told by my daughter that "Ann is in Daddy's bed." I may have been guilty of adultery, but Lawrence and I never slept together in the presence of my children before we were married. I know that comment sounds like the pot calling the kettle black. But the boundary of sexual propriety was important to me. The fact that Sam flaunted his sex life in front of our young children confirmed to me how little he really cared about them.

As soon as Lawrence and I could arrange our professional lives, we took jobs back in Tennessee in order to be with my other two children. After all, since I would no longer be living in DC -- the basis for the judge's custody ruling -- there would be no reason for the children not to live with me and their new sister. I must have been delusional. I called Sam, told him that we were moving back, and asked him to consider how we could work out the joint custody arrangement. Sam's answer was to marry a woman whom he had dated for thirty days (she had been our neighbor when he and I were married) and to sue me for sole custody. Sam also told me if I tried to see my children when I returned to town, he would have me arrested. And he meant it.

It took a year to have the custody case heard. A special judge from out of town was brought in to hear the case. This time I lost because I worked. The judge ruled that because Sam's new wife did not work and could pick up the children when school was out in the afternoon, that Sam's home was the better place for the children to live. The judge also awarded Sam full custody of my children and told me I could see the children every other weekend and for two hours on Wednesday nights, beginning thirty minutes before I got off work. When my attorney pointed this out to the judge and asked if the Wednesday night visitation hours could be pushed back to allow me to leave work and then have the full two hours for visitation, the judge refused.

Sam did everything he could to prevent me from being involved in my children's lives, both before that second trial and after he was awarded sole custody. If there was a school event he made sure I did not know about it. He went so far as to instruct the children's schools and teachers not to talk to me. He even instructed the pediatrician not to divulge any medical information to me.

I learned a lot about the ugly side of people during this time. Most particularly, I learned what it was like to be shunned. Hester Prynne had nothing on me. I might as well have been wearing a scarlet A. One time I was in the grocery store and looked up to see a woman I knew coming toward me pushing her buggy. When our eyes met she turned her back and walked the other way. It happened to me at my son's sporting events. On more than one occasion when I would say hello to someone I knew -- and this was always a woman -- the person would stare at me and then deliberately make a point of turning her back on me. There is no telling what my ex-husband had said about me. Or maybe they were just afraid of associating with me.

The most hurtful of these shunnings involved a woman who I thought had been my friend. We had spent a lot of time together because we were neighbors and our children were the same age. After I returned to Tennessee I called Margaret. I was looking forward to seeing her and wanted to set up a time to meet for lunch. While we were talking, Margaret's husband kept picking up the telephone. I could tell from the increasing agitation in Margaret's voice that she was getting nervous about being on the phone with me. A few days later I received a letter from Margaret. She told me she wished me well, but that her husband had forbidden her to have any contact with me. She asked me not to call her again. And so it went. None of the people in Sam's social circle even acknowledged my presence. I was anathema.

I have to wonder if their actions had anything to do with my choice of second husband. I left a man from a wealthy and prominent family for a man who had neither social status nor a large bank account. Such a choice was unfathomable to people whose lives were measured solely by money and position. It frightened the men because it made them potentially vulnerable to losing their trophy wives to the sort of man they had never before considered to be a threat. It frightened the wives because they saw that their husbands' wealth and power could rob them of their children. I was like a contagious disease. Although these were the same people with whom I had socialized while Sam and I were married, many of whom I had considered actual friends, I was now considered too dangerous. They cut me from their lives as surely as if I had been a cancerous growth.

With the loss of my two older children, life became almost unbearable. Even marriage to a man I loved and the birth of an adorable daughter could not assuage the searing and cutting gash in my soul. So I started drinking. I had to anesthetize the sharp edge of pain in order to survive. I truly believe that had I not been able to dull the pain with alcohol, I would have committed suicide. I still functioned professionally, and had you been around me at any social event, you would never have had the slightest indication that I had a problem with alcohol. I did my drinking at home and in secret.

Women become alcoholics much more quickly than do men. It is well documented scientifically that women cannot metabolize alcohol in the same manner and at the same rate as can men. Even though I was drinking only wine, in short order I became a daily drinker, and within five years' time had crossed the line into active alcoholism. I looked good, had a good job, had never had a DUI, had never had any outward consequences from drinking. But I could not stop drinking.

We stayed in Tennessee for about two years after Sam was awarded sole custody of my two older children. During that time, Lawrence watched me slip further and further into depression and alcoholism. He also watched Sam do everything he could to hurt me. When Lawrence was offered a position as a federal administrative judge in another state, he told me that we had to leave. Lawrence told me he was worried about my sanity if we stayed in Tennessee.

Now, almost twenty years later, I know that we made the right decision in leaving Tennessee and moving to Mississippi. Five months after arriving in Mississippi I stopped drinking and joined Alcoholics Anonymous. I started that long road of recovery and self- examination. Self-examination is like peeling an onion. The removal of each layer reveals yet another layer. When we look at ourselves, at our own character defects, at what motivates us, at what hurt us, at what has made us who and what we are, we can do it only one layer at a time. It would be too overwhelming to do it all at once. As goes the saying in AA, "progress, not perfection." And so, I began peeling the onion.

Evil Is as Evil Does

With each peeled layer, I became better equipped to help my two older children as they dealt with the unraveling of their father's professional and personal life. As I wrote earlier, my ex-husband Sam was angry about having to work for a living instead of enjoying the fruits of his family's chain of businesses. He had grown up in a wealthy household where money had not been a particular issue, nor a deterrent to whatever he had wanted to do. Life had not worked out the way Sam had anticipated, nor the way his new wife had anticipated. She thought she was marrying money, but within a few years of their marriage Sam had run through all of his trust fund money – and both he and his wife were incapable of living on the income he earned as a stockbroker.

Sam couldn't expect his new wife to work. After all, the fact that she didn't work was the reason he had been awarded sole custody of our two children. He could not risk opening that door. Secondly, his wife had no marketable skills. She couldn't bring in enough money to make a difference even if she could find a job. Further, his wife had no intention of working. None of her friends worked, and she wasn't going to, either – working would interfere with her tennis games and lunches out with the girls.

Eventually things got so bad financially that the bank started foreclosure proceedings against their house. Sam got enough money from somewhere to stop the foreclosure proceedings, and was able to keep the house. But he also started down a road which would eventually lead to the loss of his broker's license and near-bankruptcy.

Before my older daughter came to live with me she had attended a private school.

Sam's financial condition became so tenuous that he was unable to pay her tuition. Several times in the two years that my daughter attended that school, she would come within a day or so of being expelled for non payment of tuition. At the last minute Sam would come up with the exact amount needed to keep my daughter enrolled. When my son became old enough to enroll at that same school, Sam told my son that he was not smart enough to be accepted at that school. This was a lie. The board of trustees had rejected my son's application because of his father's bad credit, and had sent a copy of the denial letter to me. What kind of loving parent tells a child that he is stupid just so the parent doesn't have to face reality? When my son was finally accepted into that school, it was only because his grandmother was paying his tuition.

My children spent alternating major holidays and each summer with me in Mississippi. When it would be time for the children to return to Tennessee my older daughter would become very upset. She did not want to leave me. She had never wanted to live with her father, and the older she got, the worse her life with him became. My daughter would cry upon arrival at her father's house, whereupon Sam and his wife would berate her for crying and for being ungrateful for the "wonderful life" that her father was providing her. As my daughter grew older she began to ask Sam to let her live with me. His answer was to grab her, drag her up the stairs and scream at her that if she left "him" he would make sure she never saw her brother again.

How my daughter ever gathered the courage at age fourteen to leave her father is a question that neither she nor I can answer, even now, thirteen years later. When Sam figured out that my daughter was actually going to leave his home, and that she was of the legal age to decide which parent she wanted to live with, he locked her and her brother in the car, drove them around town for two hours, and told them every terrible thing he could about me. I don't think Sam thought he would change our daughter's mind about moving. I think he did it out of pure meanness.

The absolutely most evil thing that Sam did to either of our children was done to my son. After my daughter moved to live with me, Sam told our son – who was then eleven years old – that if he moved to Mississippi to live with me like his sister had done that he would kill himself. I found out about this because my son asked me if I thought his father might commit suicide. When I asked him what would make him ask such a question, he told me what his father had said to him. What kind of a parent says something like that to a child?

Eventually Sam lost his job. He had used my son's social security number to take advantage of unauthorized stock trading. He could have been criminally prosecuted.

He was not. However, in addition to being fired he lost his broker's license and became virtually unemployable in the financial field. Sam remained unemployed for the next several years, during which time he was supported financially by his sister, who, true to form, had married not only one, but two wealthy older men. By the time Sam died, he was completely destitute.

I firmly believe that to a great extent our actions and our thoughts affect our physical well-being. It is also well-known in medical and scientific circles that when our bodies are kept under stress for extended periods of time, we can actually damage our immune systems. Sam lived a bitter and hateful life. He was selfish, self- centered and cruel. And at the age of forty-nine, he was diagnosed with metastasized end stage melanoma. They never found the primary spot. He was dead in nine weeks. I believe his emotional life so compromised his immune system that his family's genetic predisposition to melanoma was able to take hold and quickly kill him. He died a painful and bitter death, the result of a hateful and bitter life.

I am sorry he lived as many years as he did. I am sure that no one is the perfect parent, and all of us make mistakes. But Sam was truly one of the "people of the lie" that Scott Peck writes about in his book of the same name. Sam was constitutionally incapable of being honest with himself. He was never able to look at his role in the demise of our marriage because he was never able to look at his own emotional baggage. I think it was simply too potentially painful, so he shut the door on all of it. Instead, he crafted an elaborate version of our marriage which cast him as the hapless victim. Eventually he even believed his own lies. As with the people of the lie that Peck writes about, Sam was willing to sacrifice his children's mental and emotional health so that he could maintain the illusion which ultimately became his reality. I am sure that the way I left that marriage harmed my children. I accept responsibility for that fact, and understand that both my children and I have paid a great price as a result. However, nothing can compare with the emotional wounds inflicted on my children by their father. Those scars are the ones my children will carry for a lifetime.

Emasculation

Just as my grandmother had emasculated my father by binding him to her emotionally and financially, so too did my father repeat that dynamic with my brother. As I have written, my father ruled all of us with an iron fist, but with my brother he also added the element of illusion. In real life, when a nineteen- or twenty-year-old man gets married and has children, he is expected to step up to the plate, so to speak, and accept responsibility for himself and his family. He gets a job, and if he wants to continue with an education he works and goes to school at night. Hundreds of thousands of people do this every day. The illusion my father offered my brother was this: as long as my brother permitted my father to direct my brother's life, my father would provide my brother with a standard of living which would allow him to live a fantasy in which he was both educated and financially successful.

In my parents' marriage there had been three persons – my father, my mother, and my grandmother. So too were there three people in my brother's marriage – my brother, his wife, and my father. My father's relationship with his own mother had been very much one of husband and wife, even though he was married to my mother. This is not to say that there was anything sexual between my father and his mother. I do not believe that there was any such thing. But, there was an unhealthy emotional intimacy between my father and his mother that effectively prevented my parents from having a true marital relationship with each other. The relationship between my father and my brother was likewise emotionally unhealthy. My father could not let my brother be a man because if my brother became a man, my father would no longer have any control over my brother's life. My father's need for control was almost as strong as his need to be a martyr. Those two needs best defined the parameters of my father's life and the reasons for his actions. When I escaped my father and his control, he tightened his grip on my brother.

Of course my father blamed Dan's wife for all of my brother's problems. After all, she was Catholic and she had tricked my brother into marrying her by getting pregnant. It was her fault that my brother never finished college. It was her fault that my brother never had any money. It was her fault that my brother was fired from jobs, and it was her fault that my brother's business failed. This extensive litany of blame was a song my parents constantly sang for my brother. My parents, but particularly my father, absolutely refused to assign any responsibility whatsoever to Dan for his financial, personal, and business problems. And because my parents perpetuated this myth for my brother, Dan saw no reason to accept responsibility for himself. None of his problems were his fault.

One of the side effects of the relationship between my father and my brother was – no surprise here -- the eventual estrangement of my brother from his wife. Dan's wife tried a variety of behaviors aimed at getting my brother's attention, including on one occasion actually setting the house on fire in a tiff of anger. All my brother did in response was haul his two youngest children -- grammar school age at the time -- into the burning kitchen to tell them to take a look at their "crazy mother." When throwing china and tearing up furniture had no effect, Dan's wife decided to look elsewhere for attention. She began frequenting bars and began a series of extramarital affairs. My brother knew all about them. In fact, he had a public brawl with one of his wife's lovers in the parking lot of the local grocery store near their home. However, instead of trying to mend his relationship with his wife, Dan's pat lament was, "Why won't she be an obedient wife like the Bible says she should be?" I guess my brother never got the concept of free will when he was attending church.

As you might have guessed by now, the real victims of this insanity were my brother's children. Because both Dan and his wife were basically self-centered children themselves, regardless of their chronological age, they were incapable of raising children who had any kind of boundaries or rules. The children were completely undisciplined. One time when the oldest boy was in high school he decided he wanted some khaki shorts. He went into my brother's closet, took out several pairs of Dan's dress khakis, and cut them off for shorts. When my brother discovered this he attacked his son and tried to strangle him. My sister-in-law had to call the police.

The children were moved from one school to another because my brother was perpetually in arrears in paying their tuition. Generally by the time my father stepped in to pay, the schools had already expelled the children. All the late payment did was to prevent Dan from being sued for the tuition. The only child who completed six years in the same school was the son Dan had named after our father. My father paid almost all of the six years' worth of private school tuition to send that boy to the school my father and brother had attended. None of the other three children ever finished high school. Neither my brother nor his wife pressed the issue. Two of those three were still living at home in their twenties, neither working nor attending school. They were well on their way to repeating my brother's life, except that my brother did not have the money to support them. He was still trying to get money from my father to support himself.

Dan never could understand why his life was the way it was. Once he asked me how I could have such a nice home and be financially secure. I replied that I had finished college, obtained a law degree, worked hard for over twenty-five years, saved money, and lived within my means. He just looked at me. He then began to tell me about all the people who had worked for him, or for whom he had worked, who had "screwed him over." Dan blamed them for his business failures. In all of his talking over all the years, it was always someone else's fault that he did not get a piece of business, or he lost a job. It never occurred to Dan that completing his education, working hard, saving money, and living within his means might have made a difference. And, frankly, while being fiscally responsible would certainly have helped my brother's living situation, money alone would not have solved his problems.

When my father died, things became very difficult for my brother. I am sure I do not know about every penny my father gave to my brother, but I do know that he gave Dan several hundred thousand dollars over a period of fifteen or twenty years. My father kept immaculate records. A few years before my father died, he fell off a wall and had temporary speech and writing impairments. My mother asked me to review my father's papers in the event that he did not recover. My father had documented all the money he had given to Dan. How much additional money my father gave my brother in the three or fours years after that event and before my father died of cancer, I am not sure. When my father learned he was dying he started destroying his records.

As I have said, the last money my brother received from my father was the money he stole from my father's wallet within an hour or so of my father's death. Within four months of my father's death my brother was once again fired from a job. After being unemployed for almost a year, Dan had been hired for a sales position by a company in a nearby state. Dan never relocated even though it was a job requirement. Instead, he drove back to Chattanooga each Friday and back to work on Monday. Even though he was given a serious warning by his employer about these attendance problems, Dan ignored the warnings. He actually told his employer that he was not being paid enough. In my brother's mind, being a mere salesman was beneath him. He should be at least a regional sales manager, supervising others and getting a cut of their sales. Dan could not understand why his employer failed to appreciate what my brother thought were his obvious talents.

My brother's stated reasons for his weekly return to Chattanooga was his claim that his children needed to see him and that he had other business to take care of in Chattanooga. Of course, the children who "needed" him were young adults and the "business" that he allegedly needed to take care of was his fantasy millionaire business. Dan's marriage was in such bad shape by this time that when he came home on the weekends his wife would stay somewhere else. In reality, his children did not need him, there was no other business to take care of, and his wife couldn't even stay in the same house with him.

So, after months of showing up for work only three days out of five, missing mandatory sales meetings and failing to meet his sales quotas, Dan was fired. True to form, in my brother's mind, none of this was his fault. He told me that he had worked for unscrupulous people who had hired him under false pretenses and then had sold the business out from under him. Amazing.

After losing this last job, Dan made no real attempt to look for work. Instead, he began calling my mother for money. By this time my mother was in a residential assisted living facility due to her significant physical impairments. Dan would call her asking for money to have his children's teeth pulled (the youngest was nineteen by this time), money to pay for a new heat pump for his house, and finally money to keep his house from being foreclosed. Dan told my mother that his family could not understand why she would not help them. Nothing like playing the guilt card.

This continued for months. Finally, Dan told my mother that she did not need to be in the assisted living facility, that I should buy a house for her so that he could move down to Mississippi to live with her, and that he would take care of her. Even my mother understood what that was all about. Since my brother was going to lose his house, he would just move to Mississippi, live with my mother, and be supported by her money. To her everlasting credit, she told him no.

Periodically Dan would turn his attention to me. Eventually Dan told me that I was the cause of his current financial problems because I had refused to give him money for his bills. He would rant at me (yes, he had inherited that lovely trait from my father) because I would not move Mother into my home with me, telling me that he and his preacher did not approve of warehousing in nursing homes and that I was wasting "his inheritance" by paying for mother to be in a private pay facility with full-time companions. Eventually I stopped taking his calls or reading his emails.

Dan's behavior was, of course, the logical end result of the malignant relationship he had with my father for almost fifty years. However, as bad as was the damage that my father inflicted on my brother, fault cannot rest solely at my father's feet. My mother willingly participated in blaming others, most particularly Dan's wife, for my brother's problems. And Dan was the willing victim, because to have done otherwise would have required my brother to accept responsibility for his life and the consequences of all of his choices.

The decision to be responsible for oneself is a choice. If we have done our work, if we have felt our pain, if we have looked at ourselves honestly, we eventually peel enough of the onion to begin to grow up emotionally and to accept responsibility for our actions. The ability to take these steps requires at least a modicum of maturity. Even as badly damaged as my brother had become, he could have taken those first steps if he had so chosen. He did not. Instead, he retreated more and more into a delusional world of his own making. Eventually my brother's comments, actions, and assertions became so bizarre that I began to question his hold on reality. At one point I even bought a gun and learned how to shoot it because I was afraid of what he might try to do in a fit of anger. Desperate people do desperate things, and in my brother's mind I had become the reason for all of his problems simply because I would not give him any money.

The Burning Bush

I had never been much of a drinker. I did not start drinking until college, and then drank only infrequently. I really did not like the taste of alcohol and I did not like the feeling of inebriation. In retrospect, I see that the first warning signs indicating my intolerance for alcohol occurred when I was in law school and discovered wine. I began to develop a habit of drinking too much at one time. I seemed to be missing that internal control which tells a normal drinker when enough is enough. Alcoholics will recognize the sign. It's the inability to stop after that first drink that causes the problem. Still, until I hit my emotional Armageddon, I was able to control my drinking, and for the most part, to drink like normal people.

The loss of my children in my divorce nearly killed me. Literally. The emotional pain was so debilitating that I could barely function. I wept constantly. I felt as if a part of me had been ripped from my body. Each morning when I awoke I prayed that I was waking from a nightmare. I was not.

I remember that it was about this time that the movie *The Color Purple* came out. Lawrence and I went to see it. In the movie, the character played by Oprah Winfrey has her children taken away from her. As I watched Winfrey's character collapse in agony I was so reminded of my own loss that I became hysterical and had to leave the theater. I stood in the women's restroom for what seemed like hours with my fist in my mouth, trying to stop the heaving sobs which were undulating, out of control, throughout my body. I felt like I was dying. To this day I cannot watch that movie. It is simply too painful.

Six months after Lawrence and I married, I became pregnant. I was so happy. I was also worried because I knew I was drinking too much. In fact, by the time I got pregnant I had become a daily drinker. I could "maintain" at work, but when I returned home each evening to a house without my children, the unbearable pain would quickly resurface. I learned that a glass or two of wine would take the edge off the pain. Soon, I could not face the evening without it. It was only by sheer force of will that I was able to restrict my drinking during my pregnancy to three glasses of wine a week. I was so angry that Lawrence was able to drink as much as he wanted for those months and I was not. Alcohol made everything seem better and I wanted it badly. I am just grateful that during my pregnancy I was still at a point in my disease where I could control my drinking.

After our daughter Lucy was born we moved back to Tennessee in order to be with my other two children. It did not turn out the way I had hoped. As I told you earlier, instead of being able to work out a joint custody arrangement with my ex, I ended up completely losing custody because my ex had married a stay-at-home wife. As Sam aptly informed me, he "had a new mother."

The judge's ruling was the nail in my coffin. But for the fact that suicide would have made Sam the ultimate winner, and would have truly devastated my children, I would have taken that route and ended my pain. Since it was not a viable option for me, I chose the only other option I thought I had. I increased my alcohol consumption so that I would feel nothing, and within a year or maybe less had crossed the line from abusing alcohol to full-blown alcoholism.

I did not think I was an alcoholic. The only alcoholics I knew were people who began drinking at 8:00 in the morning and were passed out by dinner time, and that certainly did not describe me. I knew I had a drinking problem, but I had never had a DUI, I had never passed out, I wasn't living under a bridge, I was on the fast track professionally. I never drank more than two or three drinks at any social function. No one except Lawrence knew how much I was drinking or that I had a problem with alcohol.

I had no outward consequences at all from my drinking. All of my consequences were internal. By the time we moved to Mississippi my internal life was black. No joy. No light. No feeling. No life. All I cared about was making sure I had enough wine to drink from the time I got home from work until I went to bed. I had night sweats each night and woke with a dull headache each morning. I swore each morning that I would not drink that day, but within fifteen minutes of walking in from work I had a glass of wine in my hand. I drank steadily each night until I went to bed.

Even though I could not stop drinking, I still did not think I was an alcoholic. What finally got my full attention was when I realized I was beginning to lose my mental functioning ability. The realization that something was happening to my mind scared the living daylights out of me. I still did not think I was an alcoholic. But I knew I could not stop drinking, even though I wanted to, and that it was going to kill me by taking my mind.

I had been raised in a "Christian" home to the extent that we went to Sunday school (not church) each week and said a blessing over our meals. That was about it. I don't think I ever heard my parents or any of my religious teachers ever tell me that God was a god of love. To the contrary, I was taught that I had better act right because Divine punishment would be swift for my various sins. It was no surprise that the view I developed of God was of a Supreme Being who was waiting around the corner of my life to beat the shit out of me when I made a misstep or broke a rule.

To this day I don't know what made me send that prayer to a God I thought would only punish me. But on the night of April 15, 1990, as I lay in my bed, I asked God to relieve me of the compulsion to drink. And He did. I actually felt a physical weight lift from my body. I had what is known in Alcoholics Anonymous as a burning bush experience. Whatever name is given to what occurred that night, there is no doubt in my mind that I experienced a miracle of healing.

The healing that occurred that night was the beginning of a new life for me. Within a week I met a spiritual healer who directed me to AA. I began attending AA meetings on a regular basis, and eventually began the long, tedious, and painful task of introspection with a therapist. I made amends to those I had harmed. I became more aware of others, and tried to do the next right thing whenever possible. I also found a spiritual life that has increased in depth and intensity over time. I seldom go to church, but I am in conversation with God on a daily basis. Life is not perfect, and neither am I, but I am content, and I live in abundance. All of these blessings are the direct result of God's grace, the shared experiences of my fellow travelers on the road of sobriety, and the layers uncovered in peeling the onion.

And I have needed all the help I could get, because my family of origin continued to be crazy.

The Sins of the Father

The Biblical assertion that the sins of the father are visited on their children is absolutely correct.

When I read that particular scripture, I thought it was grossly unfair. Why should children be punished for what their parent has done? It was not until I started peeling my own onion that I realized what that particular scripture meant. And although I have never studied any other religious treatises, I am certain that this truism is found in the religious books of every major religion, because it is an immutable fact of life.

What were my father's sins? Remember, my father had been emotionally abandoned by his own father and he had been a victim of his mother's emotionally incestuous relationship with him. As a result he had sexual identification issues which affected his relationship with my mother, and, more significantly, affected his relationship with my brother. Just as my father had been allowed only the role assigned to him by my grandmother, so too my brother would be assigned his life role by my father. My father was determined that my brother would become an athletic superstar, thereby affirming my father's maleness vicariously. Unfortunately, once my brother became that superstar, my father could never let him fail, because my father believed my brother's failure would reflect negatively on him. Preventing Dan's failure by supporting my brother and his family financially gave my father absolute control over my brother, but it also had a most unfortunate side effect. Because Dan never had to face the financial consequences of his actions, he saw no reason to change his behavior. Instead of growing into a man, my brother willingly remained dependent on my father.

The price my brother paid for turning over his life to my father was the destruction of his own children. Just as my brother was never made to accept responsibility for his own actions, so too were his own children never made to accept responsibility for themselves or to suffer the consequences of bad choices. Of all the sins Dan visited upon his children, and there were many, the failure to allow his children to suffer the consequences of their actions is the one from which they may not be able to recover.

The oldest boy, the one who also cut up Dan's dress pants, did not like wearing braces on his teeth. So, he took a tool to them and literally ripped them off his teeth. My brother just threw up his hands. That same boy was expelled from one school after another for academic failures. Instead of confronting his son with a consequence of his failure to attend to his studies or to explore any possible medical or mental reasons for his son's academic difficulties, my brother simply blamed his wife. When that son was arrested for trespassing and destroying thousands of dollars of property at the local golf club, my brother retained one of our cousins, a local attorney, and asked him to call in a few favors so the charge could be reduced to a misdemeanor without jail time. My brother never paid the legal fee to our cousin and his son never paid any consequence for his actions. I could go on and on. Suffice it to say that the oldest son repeated his father's early life by marrying early himself, having a child, not getting an education and being barely employable. He, his wife, and his young child live with his wife's parents. Absent a life-changing event of some sort, the future does not look good for him.

The second son has been damaged even more than his older brother. In addition to dropping out of high school, son number two suffered from drug problems. Of course, my brother refused to acknowledge this fact even when son number two was arrested for driving the wrong way on a major street in the middle of the night, dragging a tree which was lodged under his car. Son number two was so impaired that he did not know he had run over the tree. Once again, my brother hired our cousin, who was able to negotiate a reduced plea with no jail time. My brother was furious. He claimed the drug test results were false, that his son never took drugs, and he was livid at our cousin because any kind of plea meant that son number two had a criminal record. At the hearing, Dan verbally accosted the arresting officer, accusing him of "picking on" his son, and avoided arrest himself only by the intervention of our cousin. The only person who suffered any consequence in this scenario was my poor cousin. True to form, my brother refused to pay his legal fees.

As a result of the plea, son number two lost his license, and eventually his car. Since that event, son number two has lived at my brother's house doing absolutely nothing.

He is now in his mid-twenties and has neither a high school diploma nor a GED. He does not have a job. My brother's excuse for son number two being unable to work or go to school is because he has no car. When my mother pointed out to Dan that her grandson could ride the bus to work or school, my brother retorted indignantly that only maids rode the bus. To which I have to say, at least the maids know how to work.

The youngest child, a daughter, has followed in the footsteps of the oldest two by dropping out of high school and living at home doing nothing. During her junior high and high school years she went to a different school every year. Either Dan's failure to pay tuition or her failing grades necessitated a yearly move. It was impossible for the daughter to develop any stable and lasting friendships. Finally, at the beginning of her senior year of high school she just quit. She made one attempt at a community college where she could have obtained a high school certificate, but dropped out during the first semester. Now, like son number two, she lives at my brother's house, unemployed and uneducated.

Only the son named after my father, son number three, has so far escaped. That child alone has graduated from high school and is attending a small out of state college on an athletic scholarship. Of course, son number three was the only child with any semblance of stability in his life, due primarily to the fact that he was able to stay in the same school from the seventh grade through high school graduation because either my father or men who felt sorry for my nephew paid the boy's tuition.

It must be noted that just as my mother was a silent participant and co-conspirator with my father in his treatment of my brother, so too was Dan's wife a willing participant in the neglect and abandonment of the children she had with my brother. I really don't know why my sister-in-law had any children to begin with. She totally abdicated her parental duties. She did not work outside the home, nor did she expect to work inside the home taking care of the children or the house chores. She told my brother it was his responsibility to support her and his children. In addition to doing the grocery shopping, cleaning the house, and washing the clothes, she expected my brother to fix dinner and to bathe the children when they were younger. Since she did not work outside the home, nor did she take care of her home or her children, I can't imagine what my sister-in-law did for twenty-five years, other than blame my brother for all of the family's financial problems, and repeatedly tell her children what a failure their father was. It was a sick dynamic that fed both my brother and his wife.

I think the Biblical assertion that the sins of the father are visited upon the children is actually an understatement. If my brother's situation is typical, the more correct assertion would be that the sins of the father are visited on the children exponentially from one generation to the next. My brother was damaged by my father who had been damaged by his own parents. My brother, in turn, damaged at least three of his four children, with the damage to son number two likely irreparable. And, son number one, married with a child, no education, and no prospects of decent employment stands on the cusp of passing the damage to his own son. With each generation, the downward spiral has begun earlier and with more rapidity. And so it will continue until the cycle is broken.

Never Good Enough

I don't remember when I first understood that I was lacking in my father's eyes. It must have been when my brother started his sports life and my father began ignoring me fairly regularly. In truth, the only time I had my father's undivided attention was when he was giving me a paddling. Otherwise, he just wasn't interested in what was going on with me.

That did not deter me from trying. Throughout my growing-up years I did all that I could to be noticed. I made excellent grades, I was elected to the right clubs in school, and invited to membership in the right social societies. I dated the right boys, and I never got in trouble of any kind. I was the perfect child. I have written of the difficult time during my first year of college. However, I recovered from that episode and quickly returned to the perfect child mode. I finished college and law school and obtained a good job in the right law firm. And I married well.

Although my parents were initially overjoyed when I married my first husband because of his social status and family money, well before the time that Sam and I actually divorced, my parents had changed their minds. I was never certain of the reason for this about-face. I think it had to do, in large part, with the fact that the longer we were married, the more apparent it became that Sam was absolutely spoiled rotten and completely lazy. It was all right for my brother Dan to be spoiled and lazy, but not so my husband. Maybe Sam's behavior and character defects reminded my parents too much of my brother's failings. Too close for comfort, as the saying goes. At any rate, my parents were coolly cordial to

Sam, saving their undisguised feelings to be vented on me in private. When Sam and I divorced, their sentiment was "good riddance." And they never ceased to remind me what a bad choice I had made in marrying Sam to begin with.

Actually, I knew I was making a mistake on the day of my wedding. I had a huge wedding because it was expected and because it made my father look good: a formal evening wedding with five hundred guests, and a country club reception (my father used someone else's membership) with an open bar. Big doings. I remember walking up the steps of the church in my wedding dress and thinking, "This is wrong. I should not be doing this." But I was a coward. There were five hundred people sitting inside the church and I had all those presents. How could I possibly back out now? So I went down the aisle to my waiting fiancé and his father, both of whom were totally inebriated. They had been drinking not only since the wedding brunch that morning, but up to the time they walked in the door of the church. To this day I am surprised the pastor went ahead with the service. The next morning when I woke up as a married woman I thought to myself "Well, I am totally fucked now" - and I didn't mean it in a good way. It took me seven years of hell to find the courage to leave that marriage.

My parents were never satisfied with my choice of husband number two. Lawrence came from a poor family. He was the first in his family to go to college and the only one ever to obtain a professional degree. In addition to being poor, Lawrence had the misfortune, in my parents' eyes, of having a mother who was Spanish (a foreigner) and Catholic (a heathen). When my parents realized I was going to marry Lawrence, they went ballistic. Never mind that I was thirty-three years old and was not asking their permission. They told me I was marrying beneath myself. In their world there was no greater sin. How could I do this to them? I might have been excused for having left my first husband if it had resulted in my marrying well the second time. But, marrying a man from a poor family who was half foreign was simply unheard of. My mother became so distraught that she actually wrung her hands and cried. It was an unbelievable spectacle.

Actually, I think if I had left my first marriage for someone my parents considered to have the right money and status, they would not have said a thing to me. This sentiment is based in fact. When I was in high school I dated a boy who eventually became an internationally ranked tennis player. This person called me off and on throughout college, even though he was in school in California and I was college in Tennessee. The calls continued even after he married.

When I was in law school, this individual came to town for a tennis event. He asked if I would go to dinner with him. I agreed. At dinner he told me that a psychic in South

Africa told him he was supposed to marry me. So, even though he was married to someone else, he asked me to marry him, even going so far as to ask me what kind of diamond I wanted. I turned him down. Later when I relayed this bizarre event to my mother and father, they were upset that I had not accepted the marriage proposal. It did not matter to them that this man already had a wife. All they saw was wealth, glamor, and stardom that I had let slip away.

Lawrence had none of these superficial accoutrements, and my parents detested him. There was no being coolly cordial to him. Although my father would never admit it, I think the real reason he did not like Lawrence was not because of Lawrence's ethnicity or lack of social standing, but because Lawrence completely ignored my father and his irrational tirades. When my father would start with one of his inane monologues Lawrence would either leave the room or call my father on his bullshit. The idea that anyone would dispute his omniscience outraged my father. I think the other thing that really got under my father's skin was the fact not only were Lawrence and I more professionally and financially successful than my brother, we were also more professionally and financially successful than my father. We were not dependent on my father or his money, and he could not control us. My father was impotent with us and he hated it.

My parents decided to punish two of my three children over my choice of husbands. Of course, the punishment was not overt, and I do not think that my children were ever aware during their growing-up years of the differences in how they were treated by my parents.

The child who escaped my parents' disdain was my oldest daughter. She had my middle name and because that was also my father's middle name, he thought she was named after him. My parents doted on her and were obvious in their preference for her. She was the grandchild who was constantly praised and who could do no wrong. They bought her special gifts and gave her money. When she graduated from law school, my mother gave her a beautiful diamond necklace. I never heard my parents say anything negative about or to that child.

My parents did not care for my son, and they were not shy about vocalizing their opinion. My son was named after his father Sam and he strongly resembled his father. The fact that my son looked like his father was reason enough for my parents not to like him. They decided, without proof of any sort, that my son must be lazy and worthless like his father. They simply could not see my son as himself – a fine and loving young man. The fact that my son graduated from college, with good grades and a good job, after joining my father's fraternity, holding a job throughout college, and working construction in the summers was irrelevant. All they focused on were my son's mistakes. In their minds, he was his father's son and not worthy of their attention. They never gave him a chance.

However, the worst treatment was saved for my last child, simply and solely because her father was Lawrence, a man my parents hated. My younger daughter was treated like the proverbial redheaded stepchild from the day she was born. When she was born, my mother told my Aunt Carol that the baby "looked funny." When presents were given at Christmas or birthdays, she was shorted. Although this third child was the smartest of all the grandchildren and a good athlete to boot, her accomplishments were never acknowledged. She was simply ignored. The irony of this was that of all my children, she was the child who most adored my parents and who loved to go to visit them when she was growing up. She said that Grandmommie and Granddaddie's house smelled cozy – the smell of my father's ever-present pipe – and she was constantly begging to go to visit them. She never saw the rejection. She only loved them. In young adulthood, despite how she was treated, this child is the one who came home from college to visit with my father when he was dying and who now regularly visits my mother when she is in town, and who writes weekly letters to her. An act of unselfish love, undeserved by the recipients.

I do not recall one word of praise from my father ever in my entire life. He never acknowledged any of my academic or professional accomplishments. He never told me I looked nice or that I had done a good job or that he was proud of me. The comments he made to me were meant to demean and to put me in my place. My mother and my Aunt Carol told me many times that I should have been the boy instead of my brother because I was the strong, independent, and successful child. I think those traits which my mother and aunt were able to identify were the very traits which -- because they were in me and not in my brother -- enraged my father. In fact, the more times my brother failed, and the worse his circumstances became, the uglier my father treated me.

The cruelest thing my father ever said to me occurred about a year and a half before he died, after he and my mother had moved to Mississippi. In consideration of my parents' inability to travel, I had invited Dan and his family to my home for Thanksgiving. About a week before the holiday, in the middle of one of his blame-fest e-mails to me, my brother announced that I "was a whore" just like his wife. My parents could not understand why I reacted so strongly to this insult. Sitting in my kitchen after eating the Sunday dinner I had prepared for him, my father said to me, "I don't know why you are so upset. What your brother said is true. You are one." Those words were a physical assault.

The fact that I had left my first marriage for another man made me a whore. Nothing else that I had done in my life made any difference. That one choice was all that mattered to my father. To this day, I don't know if my father ever understood how hateful, cruel, loveless, and demeaning he was to me when he affirmed my brother's statement. Probably not. My father was incapable of empathy or awareness of anyone else's feelings. He was a malignant narcissist, and to him I was nothing more than a Whore.

Take Care of Us

My parents had long discussed with me their concerns about my brother. Both my mother and my father told me many times that they knew they could not rely on Dan, even though he was living in the same town with them. The only time my parents heard from Dan was when he wanted money. He would not even return their phone calls unless it served his purposes.

In 2001 my mother had a slight stroke from which she fully recovered. However, two years later she had a second stroke which left her permanently disabled. Fifteen months after the second stroke, my parents told me they wanted to move to Mississippi so that they would be near me. Translation: so that I could take care of them. Being the ever-responsible daughter, I found a beautiful home for my parents, located physicians for my mother, contacted the Presbyterian church in their new neighborhood, and introduced them to the people I knew who lived near them.

My parents, however, made no effort to make friends. The few neighbors who came calling were quickly alienated by my father's penchant for monopolizing the conversation talking about himself. Neither they nor my mother could get a word in edgewise. There was no such thing as having a conversation. It was only a monologue, with my father talking about all of his wonderful accomplishments. In short order, no one came calling anymore.

The only time my parents left their house was to go to the doctor, to go to church, and to come to my home each Sunday for supper. Although their neighborhood had regular get-togethers which my mother was easily able to attend in her wheelchair, my parents were not interested. Likewise for the weekly church lunches which were two blocks from their house. They just were not interested. The reason for their disinterest quickly became obvious. My parents expected me to spend all of my spare time with them.

My refusal to put my parents first in my life infuriated my father. The fact that I had a full-time job, a husband, and a child still in high school – all of which demanded my attention – not to mention one or two needs of my own, was neither of interest nor concern to my parents. My parents expected me to visit with them on a daily basis and to rearrange my life to meet their demands. My brother jumped on the bandwagon too. Dan told me that I needed "to honor my parents" and that I was being selfish. After my father died Dan actually blamed me for my father's cancer and subsequent death. He told me if I had been "doing my job" that I would have known my father was sick and he would never have died.

As the months passed, my parents chose to become more and more isolated. Where once my father extolled the merits of Mississippi as a well-kept secret, he now began to complain bitterly about all "the niggers." The large percentage of black people in Mississippi gave my father ample fodder for daily verbal vomiting, particularly made even worse when he discovered that the editor of the state's largest newspaper was black, as was the mayor of the nearby capitol city. My father told me on a regular basis, "The day your mother dies, I am moving back to Chattanooga." He began berating my mother, blaming her for their move to Mississippi. Finally, I told them both that life was too short, and if they were really that miserable, they should move back. My father's answer? He was not spending the money.

I came to dread Sunday suppers. No one could get a word in edgewise. My father would pick one or two topics and he would rant about them from the time he entered the house until he left. Lawrence and my youngest daughter would vacate the dinner table as soon as possible. It was all either Lawrence or my daughter could do not to take exception to my father's opinions, and since both knew what rage that would evoke, they just removed themselves to avoid having to hear any of it. I, of course, just sat there with my mother and listened politely.

My mother's second stroke affected her right side. There was nothing wrong with her mind, but as a result of the stroke she was unable to dress herself, cook, cut her food, or bathe herself. My mother had initially made good progress in rehab relearning to walk, but my father's insistence on playing the martyr had disastrous results for her recovery.

My mother took water therapy several times a week at a rehabilitation hospital. My father refused to permit the aide assigned to my mother to help her in and out of the pool or to help her walk to the shower rooms to dress. The floor around the pool and in the shower room was made of tile. When tile gets wet, it gets slippery. One day while walking my mother to the shower room, my father simply turned loose of her. Of course, my mother immediately slipped on the tile floor, fell, and broke her hip. My mother had to have a partial hip replacement, and although the hip eventually healed, she was never able to regain any significant mobility. I have often wondered if my father let go of my mother on purpose.

After six months in rehab, my mother returned home basically an invalid. My father, of course, gladly assumed the role of caregiver/martyr and although he had long- term care insurance which would have paid for help for my mother, and would given my father some respite, he refused to use it. Other than eventually hiring a woman to bathe my mother three times a week, my father provided my mother's care 24/7. And it was truly 24/7 care. The stroke had affected my mother's ability to hold urine and as a result she had to go to the bathroom every two to three hours. For the last three years of my father's life until the time he got sick and I forced him to hire a full-time sitter, my father never got more than three consecutive hours of sleep.

My father had smoked cigars for twenty years or more before switching to a pipe in his sixties. He was also an inveterate coffee drinker. The man could get up in the middle of the night, microwave a cup of stale coffee, toss it down and go right back to sleep. This ability helped my father survive on very little sleep while caring for my mother. However, the combination of the physical demands of being my mother's sole caregiver coupled with my father's subsistence on nicotine and caffeine caused my father to lose a significant amount of weight. When he and my mother moved to Mississippi, he was the thinnest I had ever seen him.

In the fall of 2006 I noticed that my father really looked quite frail. Against much protesting on his part, I made him see a doctor. After the appointment he told my mother and me that he was fine and he had gotten a good report. He lied. Two months later I discovered that he had long, raw, red sores on his legs. I immediately made another appointment for him with the doctor. This time the doctor called me. When my father had gone to the doctor in the fall, his blood work had indicated possible cancer cells. The doctor had wanted my father to have a CT scan. He refused. This time, in early January 2007, he had no choice. The scans showed metastasized pancreatic cancer. My father was given six to twelve weeks to live. Treatment was not recommended due to the advanced nature of the disease.

The diagnosis had different effects on various family members. The diagnosis both devastated and terrified my mother. She had never expected to outlive my father. He had controlled her and her life for fifty-five years. I am sure she had no concept of life without him, good or bad. She was also well aware that she was incapable of independent living and she was frightened about her own future.

When my father heard his diagnosis he completely turned over the reins of his life, and Mother's, to me. This was the most startling response of all. The man who had wielded control with an iron fist relinquished that control without a word. He never even drove a car again. There was no time for me to feel anything. All of a sudden I had two elderly children completely dependent on me. There was no question in either of my parents' minds as to who would take care of them. They knew that I would. That was why they had moved to Mississippi.

When I heard the diagnosis I immediately went into planning mode. I knew what my father needed to do legally to get his house in order, and I began the implementation process. I was not sad about his diagnosis, nor was I glad about it. I was simply indifferent to it. Instead of feeling any feelings, I worked. I hired the full-time sitters, I began buying the groceries and keeping up with their medications, I took both of my parents to their respective doctors' appointments, and I paid the bills. I contacted a realtor and we listed the house. At the doctor's suggestion that my father take immediate steps to place my mother in a residential living facility, I made all the arrangements so that when my father died my mother would be cared for in the right environment for her medical needs.

My brother's response to the diagnosis was astounding. He appeared at my parents' house with yellow moving stickers and began tagging all the furniture, accessories, lamps, crystal, china, etc. and announcing that he was going to take these things. Dan actually told my parents that he intended to recreate their living and dining rooms exactly to the last detail in his own home so he could remember them. How freaky is that?

My brother wanted everything, and my parents gave it to him. They told me they felt sorry for him, and that he "really needed" those things. I had to practically grovel for my parents to agree that I could have one floor lamp, two chests, and my mother's flat silver. My father told me that getting my mother's crystal and china, items that traditionally went to the daughter in Southern families, was out of the question. All of that was going to my brother.

I did not say a word to Dan over what he tagged, even when he tagged furniture that had special meaning to me, furniture which my mother had promised to me years earlier and which I would have loved to have had in my own home. I knew it would cause an argument. My father was dying rapidly, my mother was in emotional distress, and arguing over a piece of furniture simply wasn't worth it. I regret that decision now because my brother ended up selling most of my parents' furniture and antiques so he would have money to live on after he was fired from his last job. I would have bought the furniture from him myself if I had known he was going to sell it. When he later told my mother he had sold the furniture, she cried.

I am not sure Dan ever really wanted any of the things from my parents' house. I think a large motivator was his determination that I would not get anything. Dan never could get past the fact that I had become successful, and that he had not. He could not understand why his life had turned out the way it had, much less accept responsibility for the choices and decisions he had made over the years. My brother was irrationally jealous of me, my family, and my accomplishments. The worse his life became, the more he hated me. Being able to take all of my parents' possessions was Dan's way of thumbing his nose at me. I guess it made him feel better.

The last week of my father's life was overwhelming.

As I stated earlier, the Saturday before my father died, Lawrence and I moved my parents and their sitters into a guest cottage on our property. Of course we had no idea that my father had less than a week to live. Although my brother was supposed to be in town to help us with the move, as usual he did not appear until after all the work was done.

The physical act of riding in a car and walking fifty feet from the driveway to the cottage exhausted my father. Because my father wanted to be outside, we fixed him a comfortable chair on the cottage porch. For the next four days, from sunrise to sunset, my father sat in that chair under the eaves of the porch, enjoying the moment. He thanked me for moving him and mother to the cottage. He said he just wanted to sit there and enjoy my gardens for as long as he had left.

The day after we moved my parents to the cottage, Dan arrived to supervise the packing of the furniture and other items my parents had given him so that it could be transported to Chattanooga. Up to this point, my father had not been willing to share with Dan the details of the trust my father had put in place for my mother's welfare after his death. My parents knew that once Dan realized I was going to be the trustee, and that he would no longer have access to my parents' money, Dan would be extremely upset.

"Extremely upset" was putting it mildly. My father let my brother read the trust agreement on Sunday night. On Monday morning I went over to my parents' home to continue cleaning it out. Dan appeared and began yelling at me that he didn't like what the trust said, that the trust was going to be changed and he was going to see that it was changed before he left town. When I responded that the trust was set up as our father wished, my brother's anger escalated. His face turned red, his breathing became labored, and he started toward me with his fists clenched. To be perfectly frank, he scared the shit out of me. I was alone in an empty house with a lunatic. Dan was so enraged that I really thought he was going to attack me. He was a lot bigger than me and I knew if Dan hit me I would be badly hurt.

I realized that I needed to get away from Dan as soon as possible, without antagonizing him any further, so I told him I would finish cleaning out the house later. As soon as I got into my car and headed back to my house, Dan jumped in his car and began chasing after me. I called Lawrence from my cell phone, told him what was happening, and asked him to come home as soon as he could. I was worried for my safety and that of my parents.

When I arrived at my house, my parents and the sitter were sitting on the cottage porch. I barely had time to explain to them what was happening when my brother screeched into the driveway and ran angrily up to the cottage. Dan began yelling at my father, telling him that he didn't want me to be the trustee, that he didn't like what the trust said, and that he wanted my father to CHANGE IT NOW! Finally, my dying father turned to my brother and proclaimed in a weary voice, "I'm sick of this shit! Things are the way I want them. Just shut up." I don't think my father had ever spoken to Dan like that in his entire life.

It was as if someone had ignited a rocket attached to my brother's ass. He leaped to his feet, strode into the garden, and turned on my father. Dan began keening and shrieking that "we" could not tell him what to do, and that he was leaving and never coming back. Those were the last words he ever said to my father. My brother stormed to his car and drove off. After Dan drove off, my father looked at me with a confused expression on his face and said, "What's wrong with him?"

The next day as I was driving home from work, Lawrence called me on my cell phone and told me to hurry, that my father was anxious and was asking for me. I had spent a lot of time with my father in the almost three months since he had been diagnosed, ignoring both my law practice and the rest of my family, as I understood that the time we had been spending together had become important to my father. That Tuesday night I certainly did not think that death was imminent. I just thought my father wanted my company.

As soon as I could get to the house I went out to the cottage porch to sit with my father. We held hands and simply sat in silence for quite a while. Then, because it was the right thing to do, I told him I would miss him. He told me he would miss me, too, and he thanked me again for letting him and my mother move into the cottage. He said it was peaceful at my place, and that he liked sitting on the porch and listening to the birds. When it got too dark to stay out, I walked him into the cottage and kissed him good night.

At midnight that night my father had a massive stroke. I called my brother, who was still in town and staying at my parents' old house less than five miles away, telling him what had happened and urging him to come quickly. An hour later Dan strolled nonchalantly into the cottage with a cup of coffee in his hands. He looked at me, my mother, and Lawrence, and simply sat in the closest chair, not saying a word.

For the next thirty-six hours or so we sat a death watch for my father. No one, including my father's home hospice nurse, thought he would last more than a day. He fooled us all, and we should have known better. He was in no hurry to leave this world, and even in an unconscious state, he fought to remain here. Finally, on Thursday afternoon, he was moved by ambulance to hospice. He had started bleeding into his catheter and from his mouth, and it was clear that the oral morphine we were giving him was not controlling his pain. My father died twenty-four hours later, less than a week after he and Mother had moved to the cottage.

It is hard to watch someone die in pain, even someone who has caused so much pain to others. My father died a bad death. I don't know how truly aware he was of the pain those last few days. The nurse later told me that when my father had the stroke that the essence of my father left his body. I hope so, because even in an unconscious state, with morphine patches on his body and oral morphine being administered by dropper down his throat every few hours, my father grimaced and groaned in obvious pain. Something at some level inside my father recognized the pain and responded to it. The pain was so significant that my father, even unconscious, gritted and ground his teeth to the point where his mouth bled.

The decision to move my father from the cottage to the residential hospice was a tough one. My father had wanted to die at my home, and but for the unrelenting pain he would have gotten his wish. But when the uncontrolled bleeding began from his orifices, and we were unable to give him any significant relief from the pain, I knew the right and humane thing to do was to get him to a place where higher doses of pain medications could be administered so that he would not hurt anymore.

My brother was witness to my father's suffering those last two days. Instead of being grateful that my father's death was a release from terrible pain, Dan accused me of conspiring with the hospice to hasten our father's death by overdosing him on pain medications. There was no such conspiracy but I hope the increased pain medications did hasten his death. My father's life was gone, he was not going to wake up, he was not going to be healed, and he was in obvious excruciating pain. No one with any love in his heart could have wanted my father to stay in that body any longer than necessary. If the increased pain medicines cut short my father's life by an hour or a day, and gave him relief at the end, what possible difference could it have made? My brother's lament that we were playing God was only a cover for his guilty conscience.

Reconciliation

My father and I had a difficult relationship for almost my entire life. But during his last illness we were graced with the gift of reconciliation. I must admit that the Universe certainly has a well-honed sense of irony. I would not have ever been able to accept the gift of reconciliation with my father had I not been working the program of Alcoholics Anonymous and peeling that onion for eighteen years prior to my father's illness. And I would not have been in AA had I not been an alcoholic. I would not have been an alcoholic had I not lost my children in my divorce from my first husband. And I would not have lost my children had I not made the bad choices I made trying to marry well, have money, feel better about myself, and generally to repair the emotional damage my father had heaped on me when I was a child.

I owe a huge debt to AA and its members. The gift of sobriety enabled me to take those first tentative steps toward valuing and loving myself, so that I could, in turn, value and love others. For several years in early recovery I had to limit the contact I had with my parents. The first layers of the onion were hard to peel, and it took time for me to look at what my parents had done to me, yet be able to put it in the past without anger and resentment. That is hard, hard work. Only when one can accept that regardless of what has happened in the past, each of us and only us are responsible for our present and future lives can healing truly begin. Eventually I was able to establish a different relationship with my parents, one in which I had set good boundaries and one in which I could wear my parents like a loose garment. Without recovery, and without those years of peeling the onion, it could as easily have been me rather than my brother who stood screaming at our father three days before he died.

Whatever the relationship, good or bad, it is hard to watch one's father die. My father faded before my eyes, almost on a daily basis. Even when he felt terrible, he tried to hide it from my mother. It was as if at the end of his life he finally began to see her as a separate person and to treat her with love and kindness. Hopefully, that is the person my mother will remember in her old age.

During the ten weeks from diagnosis to death I spent a lot of time with my father. It was hard for him to get comfortable, and he had very little energy. Many times I would arrive at my parents' house to find my father lying on the floor sleeping. I would put an old wool Army blanket over him and lie down beside him. We would lie like that for an hour or more. My father had lost so much weight that he was cold all the time. Even though in Mississippi the temperatures in March are in the 70s, we kept a fire going in the fireplace so my father could lie in front of the fire on a pallet. I would sit on the floor next to him to keep him company.

My father and I spent a lot of time looking at his old picture albums and reading old newspaper clippings about his career. He had saved everything. We did a lot of reminiscing. Of course he was still my father. He was still the inveterate racist, bigot, and egotist. But he was also my father and I knew I would not have him for much longer. I did not want to have regrets when he was gone.

I am grateful that I had the opportunity to spend those weeks with my father. Even though I had spent many hours over the years peeling the onion and dealing with resentments, I needed that closure with him. And, I think, he needed those weeks with me. Even knowing that death was imminent, he was never able to fully express himself with me. He never apologized for the paddlings or the way he treated me growing up, or for telling me that my brother was right and that I was a Whore. I don't think he thought he had anything to apologize for. But he did tell me, more than once, that he loved me. And even at the age of fifty-five, I needed to hear those words.

And I am grateful that my last memory of interacting with my father is that Tuesday night when we sat holding hands on the porch of the cottage, at peace with one another, listening to the early evening sounds of nature. That evening when I told my father I would miss him, I meant it with all of my being.

Epilogue

A year has passed since my father died. My mother's health is slowly deteriorating as age takes its toll on an already ravaged body. My mother is angry about the hand life has dealt her, and I completely understand. Having a sharp mind in a failing body is, as my mother says, "the pits."

My brother continues to be himself, asking my mother for money, threatening to sue me if I don't give him financial assistance, and accusing me of all sorts of malfeasance. He has not seen my mother since my father's funeral. As was his routine when my parents lived in Chattanooga, he calls my mother only when he wants something from her.

Modern medicine may well keep my mother alive for many years. I never imagined that I would be the one taking care of her. But there is no one else, and even though my mother was never there for me when I needed her, I can't abandon her now.

I learned many years ago, in the process of peeling the onion, that life must be accepted and lived on life's terms. Fighting against that fact, or wishing it to be otherwise, changes nothing. It just makes you miserable. Well before my father finally told me that he loved me, I had learned to love myself. It still hurts to think back on the painful parts of my life, but they are in the past. The past cannot be changed, and it cannot hurt me now. I have learned not to shut the door on the past, nor to regret it. The past is what has made me who I am today. And today I am a reasonably happy, physically and emotionally healthy, middle-aged woman. I live in abundance with a cup that truly runneth over. I am content and I understand the word serenity. Simply put, life is good.

When I buried my father among the jonquils and azaleas with the other sleeping dead in Forest Hills Cemetery on that beautiful day in April, I laid to rest a tormented man who had both hated and feared not only those around him, but most of all, himself. Death was a release for my father, both from the physical pain of cancer and from the emotional pain of life. My father was never able to find peace in life. Perhaps he would find it in death. And so, although I would miss him, I was glad he was dead.

LaVergne, TN USA
17 February 2011

217007LV00006B/1/P

9 781432 766375